Diasporas in America:

Negative Effects and Mitigation

A Monograph

by

Major Kristopher E. Perry

United States Air Force

School of Advanced Military Studies

United States Army Command and General Staff College

Fort Leavenworth, Kansas

AY 06-07

SCHOOL OF ADVANCED MILITARY STUDIES

MONOGRAPH APPROVAL

Major Kristopher E. Perry, USAF

Title of Monograph: Diasporas in America: Negative Effects and Mitigation

Approved by:

_____   Monograph Director
Michael W. Mosser, Ph.D.

_____   Director,
Kevin C.M. Benson, COL, AR   School of Advanced
                                        Military Studies

_____   Director,
Robert F. Baumann, Ph.D.   Graduate Degree
                                        Programs

Abstract

DIASPORAS IN AMERICA: NEGATIVE EFFECTS AND MITIGATION by MAJOR Kristopher E. Perry, US Air Force, 69 pages.

Throughout human history, people have migrated from one place to another across the globe. Since the creation of nation-states, the migration of people has been seen as emigrating from one country and immigrating to another. Immigration has recently become a vital issue for many governments throughout the world to address. The purpose of this monograph is to explore a certain type of immigration, known as "diaspora formation", specifically with respect to the United States. Historically, the word "diaspora" has referred almost exclusively to the forced Jewish population dispersion throughout the world and their eventual return to their homeland. However, in modern times, the word "diaspora" has taken on a different context altogether. Advances in technology, such as communication and transportation, as well as a worldwide economic imbalance of have's and have not's, have enabled modern diasporas to become an international force, politically and economically.

The open, wealthy societies of the West, especially the United States, have become targets for millions of people in less-privileged societies to settle in a new country, earn income to send back to the homeland, and even wield diplomatic influence within countries in which they have no intent to become citizens. The drain of money, both domestic and international, and the increasing political influence resulting from diaspora formation, is undermining the elements of America's national power. This monograph examines the negative effects of diasporas within the United States and concludes that the federal government must take affirmative steps to recognize the negative effects of diasporas and to develop an enforceable policy for dealing with diaspora formation within its borders. Without recognition and affirmative action, the United States will see its economic and diplomatic elements of national power continue to dwindle in the years ahead.

TABLE OF CONTENTS

Figures

Tables

INTRODUCTION

The old saying goes, "In 1492, Columbus sailed the ocean blue." This is a popular saying among the school children in the United States; however, the saying contains greater significance than simply a juvenile attempt to remember an important date to be tested later. In fact, the year 1492 ranks as one of the most important dates in human history. From Columbus' discovery that year of the New World would grow the most powerful nation the world has ever known: the Untied States. Today, the United States, besides having the most powerful military in the world, has many other advantages that allow it to maintain its superpower status. As of 1999, the United States had the largest gross national product of any nation; more than double that of its nearest rival, Japan.[1] By 2006, that number was more than three times that of Japan. Additionally, the US population enjoys some of the highest health and educational advantages in the world, including a life expectancy of nearly 80 years and an 85%+ high school education rate.[2] Nearly all of the population has access to clean water and sanitation, as well as free public education through the secondary level.

Today's United States is certainly not what Columbus encountered in 1492. Columbus stumbled upon a world unsettled by the Europeans or Asians, but situated squarely between the two civilizations, separated by vast oceans. In 1492, the area that is now the United States was occupied by a small indigenous population of 1.5 million. However, this belies the ethnic diversity already present within the nation. Native Americans spoke over 250 languages and had already developed a wide range of cultural adaptations to the varied environments of the nation.[3] The pre-existence of the varied Native American cultures would eventually be a harbinger of the face of the future United States.

---

[1] Immanuel Ness and James Ciment, *The Encyclopedia of Global Population and Demographics, Volume 2* (New York: M.E. Sharpe Inc., 1999), 894.
[2] Ibid, 898-899.

1

Since the days of Columbus' original "discovery" of the American continents slightly over 500 years ago, the area that is now the United States has grown from a population of 1.5 million Native Americans[4] to its current day population of 300,000,000, achieved 17 October 2006. This amounts to a 20,000% increase in only five hundred years. A simple way to determine the growth of population is by examining the birth rate, immigrant rate, and death rate to determine the rate of population growth. Currently, the United States Census Bureau uses the following markers to estimate current US population:[5]

Table 1 - Census Bureau Population Growth Rates

One birth every.....................................*8 seconds*
One death every.....................................11 seconds
One international migrant (net) every..............25 seconds
Net gain of one person every......................**12 seconds**

A quick examination of these numbers show that there is one immigrant added to the US population for every 3.2 births. In other words, immigration is currently responsible for over 20% of our population growth. Removing immigrants from the population growth rate would change net gain rate from 1 person every 12 seconds to 1 person about every 24 seconds. The impact of immigration is obvious to even the casual observer. In fact, without the immigration factor, the United States' population would grow only by approximately 1.6 million persons per year, far below that rate when immigration is included.[6] Additionally, the birth rate within the United States continues to fall due to massive demographic and lifestyle changes in modern America. As of 2000, only 1 in 3 households even had children, and the number of children per

---

[3] David Levinson, *Ethnic Groups Worldwide* (Phoenix, Arizona: The Oryx Press, 1998), 384.
[4] United States Department of State, "Portrait of the USA", http://usinfo.state.gov/usa/infousa/facts/factover/; last accessed 15 February 2007.
[5] United States Census Bureau, "USA Pop Clock", www.census.gov/population/www/popclockus.html, last accessed 15 February 2007.
[6] Geoffrey Gilbert, *World Population* (Santa Barbara, CA: ABC-CLIO, Inc., 2001), 14.

household had decreased to 2.6 children from 3.4 in 1950.[7] Without immigration, the United States could very easily find itself in an era of stagnated, or even negative, population growth.

So what is immigration and why do we care about it? Is not immigration simply something that we've always had and always will have? What happens when the immigrants only want to use the benefits of the US society, give very little in return, and eventually leave to return to their homelands? This monograph will examine the how and why of immigration to the United States, looking at immigrations of the past and present. More significantly, however, the paper will examine a largely unknown, and potentially disruptive, type of immigration, called diasporas, which is becoming more and more prevalent in American society. Finally, the paper will attempt to inform the reader of the possible negative effects of diasporas, and about how the United States should seek to mitigate those negative effects on its society.

---

[7] Cheryl Russel, *Demographics of the U.S.* (Ithaca, NY: New Strategist Publications, Inc., 2003), 282.

CHAPTER 1

On September 11, 2001, the United States was victim to some of the worst terrorist acts ever perpetrated on a civilized society. The perpetrators? All Middle Eastern immigrants of Arab descent, most of whom were in the country illegally, either with expired-visas or no visa at all. Since then, border security and controlling illegal immigration in the United States has taken center stage as a hot-button political issue impacting the nation's views on health care, jobs, security, education, culture, and population…nearly every aspect of American society. Even though, as will be seen later, immigration has always been a part of the United States, the word immigration itself has become a dirty word which evokes deep emotion from nearly all sectors of the American nation. However, immigration is a wide-ranging term that is often misunderstood, misapplied, or simply used wrongly. Before fully examining why people leave one country for another one or the potential negative impact of immigration upon the United States and how to control it, one must first understand underlying terms associated with immigration.

MIGRATION

The word immigration itself is one aspect of the broader term, migration. Migration is a natural human endeavor. It refers to the movement of populations from one area in the world to another, usually in reference to movement prior to the establishment of state and/or national borders. As Figure 1 shows, human life is widely thought to have begun in Africa and spread from there prior to the separation of the continents.[8] Human hunting pressures drove many large mammals to extinction, and human industry and cultures (including early language) evolved and diverged. Scarce resources and cultural distinctiveness further accelerated group segregation and

---

[8] "Hominid Fossil Sites", http://www.handprint.com/LS/ANC/disp.html, last accessed 15 February 2007.

interspecies competition for game, shelter and harvestable territories. This likely caused humans to migrate further and further from their point of origin.

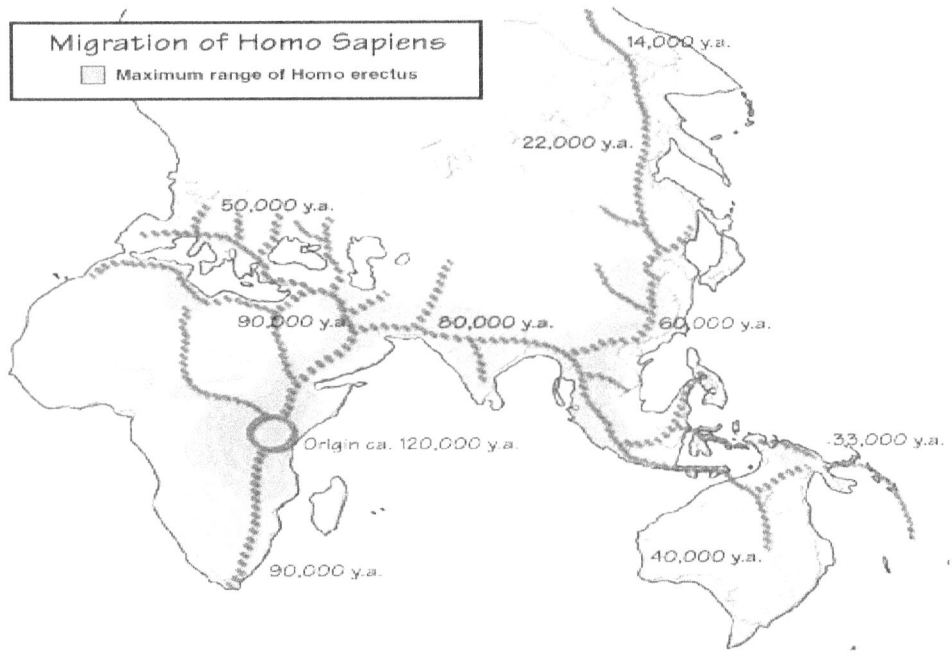

Figure 1 – Migration of Ancient Homo Sapiens

Figure 2 below shows a pictorial display of the concentrations of populations in 1800 and then projected to 2050.[9] Population explosion by birth rate explains much of what is occurring in China, Africa, and the Indian Subcontinent. However, a close look at North America on the map and the United States in particular, shows that when the decreasing birth rate is taken into account, migration of massive amounts of people to the United States accounts largely for the coming population explosion.

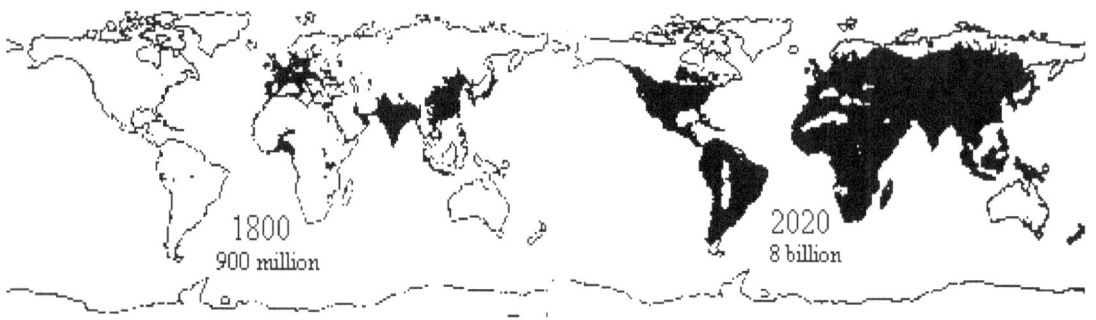

Figure 2 - Human Migration and Population Growth Since 1800

EMIGRATION

In modern times, since the establishment of states and nations, human migration is further broken down into two categories. One who migrates is either an immigrant or an emigrant, depending on perspective. Emigration is when one leaves his home nation for another. In the perspective of the home nation, this person is an emigrant: a citizen who has left the country presumably with no intent to return. Emigration can have negative effects on the home nation.

One of the most well-known negative effects of emigration is that of "brain drain". Brain drain occurs when citizens of one nation leave home to study higher education abroad and never return. Additionally, highly educated citizens from one country may emigrate from the homeland to other countries with more advantages such as increased markets, higher salaries, better standard of living, or more modern facilities. For example, the country with by far the largest brain drain in the world is Guyana, from which more than 70 percent of individuals with a tertiary education have moved to the United States.[10] Within the United States itself, Puerto Rico, an American territory, is suffering from a large brain drain to the mainland as more and more educated professionals are leaving the island in alarming numbers. The drain is taking away

---

[9] John H. Tanton, "The End of the Migration Epoch", *The Social Contract*, Vol. IV, No. 3, 1995, http://desip.igc.org/1800.html and http://desip.igc.org/2050.html, last accessed 15 February 2007.

Spanish-speaking professionals, especially doctors and dentists, to help service the growing

Hispanic population on the mainland. The *Kansas City Star* reported on October 28, 2006, that

more than 10% of registered doctors and 5% of registered dentists leave the island each year to

work on the mainland.[11]

IMMIGRATION

For every country that loses an emigrant, another country gains an immigrant.

Conventional wisdom holds an immigrant is one who enters another country, legally or illegally,

when viewed from the perspective of the receiving country, for the purpose of remaining in the

country permanently. However, in practical application, the word immigrant has many different

connotations. A quick look at the glossary of the United States government's official website of

Citizenship and Immigration reveals a cloudy picture of what an immigrant really is. In fact, the

word "immigrant" is not even defined. Instead, the reader is referred to the term "Permanent

Resident Alien", which is defined as:

> An alien admitted to the United States as a lawful permanent resident. Permanent residents are also commonly referred to as immigrants; however, the Immigration and Nationality Act (INA) broadly defines an immigrant as any alien in the United States, except one legally admitted under specific nonimmigrant categories (INA section 101(a)(15)). An illegal alien who entered the United States without inspection, for example, would be strictly defined as an immigrant under the INA but is not a permanent resident alien. Lawful permanent residents are legally accorded the privilege of residing permanently in the United States. They may be issued immigrant visas by the Department of State overseas or adjusted to permanent resident status by U.S. Citizenship and Immigration Services in the United States.[12]

---

[10] William J. Carrington and Enrica Detragiache, "How Extensive is the Brain Drain?", Finance and Development Quarterly, Vol. 36, No. 2, 1999, International Monetary Fund, http://www.imf.org/external/pubs/ft/fandd/1999/06/carringt.htm, last accessed 15 February 2007.
    [11] Miranda Leitsinger, "Brain Drain: Flight from Puerto Rico," *Kansas City Star,* 28 October 2006, sec. 1A, p. 2.
    [12] U.S. Citizenship and Immigration Services, "Glossary", http://www.uscis.gov/graphics/glossary3.html, last accessed 22 October 2007.

Immediately, a reader sees that the word "immigrant" is not such a simple term. In an attempt to put confusing legalese aside, this monograph defines an immigrant, from the perspective of a receiving country, as a person of one nationality who leaves his/her home country to take up residence in another, receiving country, either on a permanent or semi-permanent basis. This definition necessarily omits those persons who enter a country on a tourist or student visa with a definite time-frame in which they must leave the receiving country or be in violation of that country's immigration laws. However, this definition will include those persons who enter another country on work visas. The importance of this last caveat will be discussed later.

DIASPORA INTRODUCED

The United States is known the world over as the "Great Melting Pot," popularized by the play by the same name written in 1908 by Israel Zangwill.[13] because it is a nation built on immigrants seeking a new life for myriad reasons with the desire for freedom, peace, security, and prosperity. The United States has one of the most complex ethnic populations, and perhaps the most complex set of ethnic relations, of any nation in the world. Since 1492, peoples of every nation in the world have settled in the United States. The United States is, indeed, a nation of immigrants, as over 99% of all Americans were either born elsewhere or are descended from people born elsewhere. The United States has harnessed the power of its ethnic diversity to rise to its current status of superpower, the strongest nation economically, militarily, and diplomatically the world has ever known. [14]

Immigrants who legally enter a new country with the idea of becoming a permanent resident and citizen of that nation are generally recognized to be a positive force on society.

---

[13] PBS Website, "Destination America", www.pbs.org/destinationamerica/usim_qz1b.html, last accessed 10 March 2007.

Immigrants offer a receiving society a diversity of culture, ethnicity, ideas, way of doing things, ethics, and habits. By and large, immigrants who intend to stay integrate themselves into society and become productive members of that society.

However, not all immigrants to the United States have the desire to assimilate or become productive citizens of the society in which they live. Some immigrants wish to take advantage of the economic opportunities as much as they can, send as much money as they can back to their homeland, and eventually return to their homeland. These groups of immigrants are becoming more and more prevalent, especially in the United States, as people look to take advantage of the freedom and prosperity offered by the promise of the American dream, but are not willing to give up their ties to their homelands. The miniature foreign societies these people form within a receiving country are known as diasporas. It is the examination of diasporas, an analysis of the issues created for the receiving society, and ways to mitigate the negative effects within the United States with which the rest of this paper will be concerned.

---

[14] Levinson, 384, 390.

CHAPTER 2

Immigration of foreigners into the United States has been long recognized as one of our important social and political problems. Jeremiah Jenks, writing about immigration in *1926*, claims,

> "[P]erhaps no other question has aroused more bitter feelings at times, or has called out more lofty sentiments of altruistic purpose. On the one hand, our government has been besought to protect our people from the 'degrading influence' of the immigrant…On the other hand, it his been declared that our doors should never be closed against those suffering from religious or political persecution."[15]

The Jenks quote shows the immigration issue is not a new one. However, the issue of diasporas within the United States is a growing phenomenon that has many implications for the future. Before issues and solutions can be discussed, however, one needs to understand what a diaspora is, the characteristics of a diaspora and the typology of diasporas.

DIASPORA DEFINED

The term *diaspora* is derived from the ancient Greek verb meaning to "sow over." It originated from the ancient Greek tradition of migration and colonization. However, the term became almost universally associated with the dispersal and settlement of the Jews outside of Palestine following the Babylonian exile in 586 B.C.[16] In fact, Robin Cohen, a leading anthropologist in the field of diaspora study, writes, "The Jews provide the source for most characterizations of the diasporic condition."[17] The diasporic condition can be described as an ethnic community within another nation which "…denotes a persistent sense of community

---

[15] Jeremiah W. Jenks and W. Jett Lauck, *The Immigration Problem* (New York: Funk and Wagnalls Company, 1926), 2.

[16] Melvin and Carol Ember, and Ian Skoggard, eds., *Encyclopedia of Diasporas: Immigrant and Refugee Cultures Around the World* (New York: Springer Science+Business Media Inc., 2005), xiii.

[17] Robin Cohen, *Global Diasporas, An Introduction* (Seattle: University of Washington Press, 1997), xi.

between people who have left their homeland (usually involuntarily) and who may be scattered all over the world. Such diasporas…may play a crucial role in maintaining the national identity…"[18]

Recently, the term diaspora has taken on an expanded meaning and the study of diasporas has expanded well beyond the original focus on the Jews. Today, diaspora is used to refer to other major historical dispersions, many of them involuntary, such as the forced removal of the Armenians by the Turks in the early 20th century, and the forced removal of Africans by the Europeans during the 400 years of slave trade, called "The Black Diaspora" by Ronald Segal.[19] Other mass movements of population in recent times have also come to be called diasporas in the expanding modern meaning of the word. Many of these diasporas are largely voluntary for primarily economic concerns, including the mass movement of 20 million Chinese people between 1880 and 1920, most of them to the United States. Belonging to a diaspora should be self-ascribed, as assigning membership seems illegitimate if a person does not feel they are a member of a diaspora.[20] The characteristics of a diaspora which follow will expand upon the idea of membership within a diaspora.

CHARACTERISTICS OF A DIASPORA

In many of the recent population dispersals, the migrants have a strong wish to return to their homeland. They maintain ties to family and friends back home. They also may find themselves treated differently, even oppressed or discriminated against, in the receiving

---

[18] Stephen Castles and Mark J. Miller, *The Age of Migration: International Population Movements in the Modern World* (New York: Guilford Press, 1998), 201.

[19] Ronald Segal, *The Black Diaspora* (New York: Farrar, Straus and Giroux, 1995), xiii.

[20] Steven Vertovec, "The Political Importance of Diasporas", June 1, 2005, Migration Information Source, http://www.migrationinformation.org/Feature/display.cfm?ID=313, last accessed 8 December 2006.

country.[21] Because of their desire to return home, the immigrants may never fully integrate into the receiving society. Therefore, diaspora members expose themselves to a possible lack of acceptance from the society at large.

Since the word diaspora has taken on modern meaning, a list of characteristics is useful in trying to understand what a diaspora looks like when examining a particular population in the modern context. Robin Cohen, compiling his and other authors' views, offers a useful list of nine characteristics which describe diasporas:[22]

1. A dispersal from an original homeland, often traumatically, to two or more foreign regions.
2. Expansion of the homeland in search of work, in pursuit of trade or to further colonial ambitions.
3. A collective memory or myth about the original homeland, including location, history and achievement.
4. A belief that all members of the diaspora should be committed to the maintenance or restoration of their original homeland and to its safety and prosperity
5. The development, or maintenance, of a return to the homeland movement that gains collective approbation.
6. A strong ethnic group consciousness sustained over a long time, based upon a sense of distinctiveness, common history, and a belief in a common fate.
7. A troubled relationship with the host societies, suggesting a lack of acceptance at the least or the possibility that another calamity might befall the group.
8. A sense of empathy and solidarity with co-ethnic members in other countries of settlement.
9. The possibility of a distinctive creative, enriching life in the host country with a tolerance for pluralism.

This is a quite useful list of characteristics, but definitely needs further analysis to understand what is happening in today's modern world. Bear in mind that Cohen's list is neither exhaustive, nor applicable to all diasporas in its entirety. In Chapter 3 concerning diaspora formation, and Chapter 4 concerning diasporas in the United States, these characteristics will be applied to show potential points of conflict between a diaspora and its receiving country. For

---

[21] Ember, xiii.
[22] Cohen, 23-26.

now, it is useful to examine these characteristics in light of their implications for various kinds of human activities.

Writer Donald Nonini offers a way of looking at Cohen's nine characteristics by grouping them into relevance and meaning. Characteristics 1 and 2 imply a geographic mobility, at times extensive, by selected human groups. Mobility is a major factor of seeding diasporas and will be discussed in the next chapter. Characteristics 3 and 4 refer to collective processes of cultural production-the making of narratives of common origin, and creation of memories of an ideal homeland. This aids in the maintenance of the idea of the eventual return to the homeland and prevents ideological ties to the receiving country. Characteristics 4 and 5 also refer to "collective commitments" to an ancestral home to which the diasporic members will return. Characteristic 6 reminds members of the diaspora of their distinctiveness and common history.

Characteristics 7 and 9 refer to political relationships between the diasporic group and officials and leaders of the receiving country and/or the diasporic group's relationship with the other ethnic groups in the host nation. This serves an important purpose in that it prevents the diaspora members from fully integrating into the seeded society. Characteristic 8 furthers this distinction by creating a sentiment of solidarity, not with members of the receiving society, but with members of the same ethnic diaspora living in other nations. Again, this prevents members from forming an inclusive bond with members of the receiving society.[23]

Cohen is not alone in discussing characteristics of diasporas. However, nearly all of the authors researched include, basically, Cohen's characteristics in one form or another. Some authors claim fewer characteristics than Cohen's nine exist, but no authors researched have more

---

[23] Donald Nonini, "Diasporas and Globalization", see Ember, ed., 559-561.

than Cohen's nine. An example of an additional viewpoint of diaspora characteristics is supplied

by Nicholas Van Hear.[24] He proposes more minimal criteria of diasporas:

1. A population has been dispersed from their homeland to two or more other territories or nations.
2. The presence abroad is enduring, although exile from the homeland is not necessarily permanent, and may include movement between the homeland and the host nation.
3. There is social, economic, political and cultural exchange between or among spatially separated populations comprising the diaspora.

Van Hear's criteria are perhaps useful for a quick, cursory look at diasporas. For the purposes of

this monograph, a more in depth view of diasporas is needed for understanding what the United

States can do to mitigate any negative effects of diasporas. This will be discussed in detail in

Chapter 5.

Summarizing the characteristics of diasporas, diasporas begin with the mass movement of

a population being displaced from a home country into one or more receiving countries. There

must be a strong link to the home country via language, religion, or customs, preferably all three.

Usually there is a historic catastrophe or some other hardship from which people were escaping in

order to survive or better their lives or the lives of their loved ones. The tie to the home nation is

maintained through a collective consciousness that glorifies the homeland, tries to protect it, and

builds the strong desire to eventually return. These characteristics collectively aid to block or

prevent assimilation into the receiving society. Only after the characteristics of diasporas are

understood and applied a can typology of diasporas then be developed.

TYPES OF DIASPORAS

Once one determines whether or not a diaspora exists, which is no easy task, then one

needs to look to classify the diaspora into typologies. There is much debate over the types of

---

[24] Nicholas Van Hear, *New Diasporas: The Mass Exodus, Dispersal, and Regrouping of Migrant Communities* (Seattle: University of Washington Press, 1998), 6.

diasporas that exist in the world today. This is an understandable issue when viewed from the perspective of the evolution of the word "diaspora" itself. However, some general frameworks of categories of diasporas have emerged which seem to be somewhat similar. The *Encyclopedia of Diasporas*, published in 2005, has chosen to identify four distinct types of diasporas: victim, labor, trade, and imperial.[25] For his part, Cohen has identified the same four types of diasporas plus an additional type he labels "cultural". For the purposes of this paper, "cultural" diasporas will not be discussed as this type serves as a postmodern view of all diasporas in general, not a specific type of diaspora.[26] Once again, Cohen's work appears to be the most thorough discussion of the issue, and brief introduction to each of his four types of diaspora follows.

VICTIM DIASPORAS

Victim diasporas are one of two types in which the people are pushed to leave their home countries. The Jewish diaspora is the classic example of victim diasporas. The Jewish experience also serves as the most widely known and accepted definition of a diaspora. Originally, the Jewish diaspora began with Roman domination of Judea beginning as early as 6th Century B.C. The Jews were eventually almost entirely expelled from the Holy Land. However, the Jews maintained communities across the world with the idea that someday they would return to their homeland and re-establish the Jewish state. This was accomplished with the creation of Israel following the end of World War II.

Today's Jewish diaspora remains quite large, and the state of Israel even has a Department of Diaspora to maintain connectivity with Jewish communities worldwide. The numbers of Jews living abroad in diasporas are impressive, if not staggering. Keeping in mind the Jewish population of Israel is estimated at 5,300,000, there are over 5,000,000 Jews living in

---

[25] Ember, p. xiii.
[26] Cohen, p. xi, xii.

the United States, 1,000,000 in the Former Soviet Union, 500,000 in France, 400,000 in Argentina and Canada, and 300,000 in the United Kingdom.[27] Other diasporas commonly viewed as "victim" include the African slave trade with the New World, and the Armenian expulsion at the hands of the Turks beginning in 1915.[28]

LABOR DIASPORAS

Labor diasporas can be defined as those who "move across international borders to work in one country while remaining citizens in another."[29] These workers, many unskilled and uneducated, leave the homeland in search of work elsewhere. Often times in history, such as in the case of the workers from India in the 1800's, the laborers were indentured servants. Other times, especially recently, workers leave a homeland with rampant unemployment and poverty, to seek employment in other nations. The intent is to make money to support the family left behind in the homeland. These laborers are also largely unskilled workers with little grasp of the receiving nation's customs, language and tradition. The goal is simply to earn enough money to support the family back home and eventually to return to the homeland when times are better. Recent examples of this occurring in the United States include the influx of Chinese to the United States to build the railroads of the 19th and early 20th century, as well as the current-day influx of Mexican migrant workers to fill the demand for unskilled farm laborers.

TRADE DIASPORAS

Trade diasporas, in the classical world, were well documented by Homer. Merchants from one community would live as aliens in another town, learn the language, the customs, and

---

[27] Sergio DellaPergola, Yehezkel Dror, and Shalom S. Wald. *Annual Assessment 2005: A Rapidly Changing World* (Jerusalem: Jewish People Policy Planning Institute, 2006), 12.
[28] Cohen, Chapter 2.

the commercial practices of their hosts, then start the exchange of goods.[30] More recently, the

Chinese diasporas, and the Chinatowns they form, in the United States serve as the prototypical

examples of trade diasporas. Overall, the tendency of trade diasporas is to serve as a

"middleman" in the exchange of goods and services between the homeland and the receiving

nation.

IMPERIAL DIASPORAS

Imperial diasporas, nearly a thing of the past by now, were used for the purposes of

servicing and extending the empires of their home nations. In fact, nearly all the powerful nation-

states, especially in Europe, established their own diasporas abroad to further their imperial plans.

However, the British diasporas of the 17th century and later are the prime examples of imperial

diasporas. Additionally, the British emigration beginning in the 17th century was one of the

highest in volume and longest in duration in the world.[31] By 1871, there were just over 3 million

Brits living abroad, and by 1881, there were nearly 4 million British citizens living outside of the

United Kingdom.[32] There was never any intent by the vast majority of the British citizens to

remain in one of the colonies. For the most part, they continued to speak only English, and

certainly conducted all business and political transactions in English. They imported British

goods, built British style homes and schools for their families, and visited the homeland on a

regular basis. The only intent of the British citizens living abroad was to take advantage of the

host nations resources for exportation back to the homeland, all the while managing to keep as

much British identity as possible.[33]

---

[29] M. Weiner, "Labor Migrations and Incipient Diasporas", *Modern Diasporas in International Politics*, Gabriel Sheffer, ed. (London: Croom Helm, 1986), 48.
[30] Ibid., 84.
[31] Ibid., 67.
[32] Eric Richards, "British Diaspora", see Ember, ed., 47.
[33] Cohen, 75.

STRATEGIES OF DIASPORA FORMATION

Due to the relative advantages, especially economically and religiously, of living in a western, industrialized nation, they are often the target of diasporic communities. The free and open societies of western democracies and relatively relaxed immigration laws are advantageous for those seeking to establish a diaspora. While there are many ways to go about establishment of a diaspora, the methods tend to fall into four general categories: chain migration, marriage strategy, group strategy, and militant strategy.[34] A fifth strategy that is emerging especially in the United States is that of illegal migration.

Chain migration is a strategy that is most often used to settle diasporas in the west. Families will send a male member of the household, usually a son in his late teens or 20's, or perhaps the father, to a country in the west to gain asylum and establish a home. The advance migrant would find a home, get a job, and begin to save sufficient funds to cover the costs of other family members' journeys to the chosen country. Most western nations allow legal immigrants to sponsor their immediate family members into the host nation. In countries where emigration is not allowed, then the anchor member would have to save not only enough to pay for passage, but to pay some other agent to arrange to get the family out of the country safely.

A related strategy to the chain migration strategy is the marriage strategy. This strategy involves marriages of convenience between two families, many times cross-cousin marriages. The families would pool their resources to get one or both the bride and groom, into a western nation to anchor the migration. Then, when sufficient funds were obtained, the bride and groom would begin to bring both immediate families into the host nation. After which, the marriage of convenience could be dissolved quickly and easily within the host nation. Western ways of

---

[34] Christopher McDowell, "Asylum Diaspora: Tamils in Switzerland", see Ember, ed., 539-540.

divorce allow marriage to be almost effortlessly terminated. For example, the divorce rates within the United States are just over 50%, up from just under 25% only 40 years ago. [35]

A third strategy involves a group of young men from the same village, district, or school or college traveling as a group and making asylum claims on a common basis. Any such grounds, such as lack of human rights, oppression of any kind, or most any inequality, would qualify the immigrant for asylum in a western, liberal democracy. The group of men could then begin to pool their financial resources and allow for the migration of family members. In this way, the original migrants had safety in numbers and mutual support in an unfamiliar land. This would greatly ease the difficult transition to a foreign country.

A fourth strategy that sometimes shapes diasporas involves militant groups. In this strategy, militant groups fund the passage of fighters who are no longer able to fight at the front due to age or injury. The decrepit fighters would be sent to western nations to join other members of a diaspora, freeing the militants of the obligation of having to look after the incapable men. More importantly, the former combatants could be counted on to raise funds overseas, as well as support information and propaganda efforts.

Finally, the last strategy to be discussed here is that of illegal immigrants infiltrating a country by any means possible, other than legal passage. Once in the host country, the illegal immigrant can use lax immigration laws and citizenship laws to his/her advantage. One of the best ways to gain legal status within the new nation is through childbearing. Many western nations allow any child born in their borders to claim citizenship in that country, regardless of the nationality status of the parents. [36] It follows, even if the parents are in the country illegally, they would be allowed to remain to care for their infant child that is now a citizen of the host country.

---

[35] Ness, 896.
[36] Levinson, 397.

When one or more of these strategies is implemented and then repeated many times, a diaspora is

born.

CHAPTER 3

While diasporas are certainly not a new concept in world history, they do appear to be more numerous all across the world in the current day with little, if any, controls. Writer Pnina Werbner has termed this phenomenon "Chaordic Diaspora" formation because diasporas seem to be reproducing and extending themselves without any centralized command structures.[37] This is true with all migrations of people, no matter the purpose, not just with diasporas. However, modern changes in the world have undoubtedly made it easier for migration and diaspora formation. In addition, as diasporas grow larger and more numerous, the effects of them also become more apparent. The positive effects of diasporas are similar to, if not the same as, the effects of traditional migration for the purpose of permanently remaining in a new country. These positive effects will be mentioned only briefly in this paper, as positive effects are not relevant to the examination of possible threats to a society from diasporas. On the other hand, negative effects of diasporas are a very real problem in the modern world, especially for the free and open societies of the Western world. The negative effects will be examined closely in this chapter. First, however, a look at how and why diasporas seem to be forming easier and quicker in the modern world is in order.

BARRIERS TO DIASPORAS

There is no super-powerful, overlord organization which determines immigration and emigration policy for each of the over 190 nations on the planet. The United Nations is as close to such an organization as currently exists. The United Nations recognizes the right of each country to govern its own territory within its accepted borders. As such, each country is free to choose whom to let into their borders and, likewise, whom to allow to depart. However, the

---

[37] Pnina Werbner, "Chaordic Diasporas", see Ember, ed., 546.

accepted views of the international community, by and large, encourage granting the ability of people to travel freely around the world, as they wish, as long as they respect the laws of the country into which they are traveling. It is left for individual, sovereign countries to decide its own rules and regulations concerning entry of foreign citizens into its borders.

In the past, controlling entry to one's country was simple for a state's government, especially when compared to the modern day. Emigrating from one's homeland to another country was extremely difficult. In the days before the Industrial Revolution modernized transportation, one did not simply leave his home country to go to another on a whim. Ignoring for a moment the legal barriers to migration, there were many other practical barriers to be overcome before setting foot in a distant nation.

COMMUNICATION BARRIER

Traditionally, when leaving the homeland to immigrate or join a diaspora, an immigrant had to overcome many barriers. First, the emotional impact on the immigrant was extreme. He would leave everything familiar to him behind, including extended family, friends, support network, and culture. Granted, a critical characteristic of the diaspora is to maintain the connection to the homeland and the intention to eventually return, but this did not lessen the initial mental trauma of departure. Today, however, maintaining ties to the homeland is significantly easier, lessening the mental burden of departure to a new country. As Thomas Friedman calls it in his seminal book on globalization, the "Democratization of Information" via the internet and other telecommunications advances has vastly altered the communication capabilities across the planet.[38] The proliferation of the internet and other communication technologies "now make possible the 'cyber communities' or 'virtual communities' formed by

---

[38] Thomas Friedman, *The Lexus and the Olive Tree* (New York: Random House, Inc., 2000), 67.

the mediated quasi-interactions of individuals forming a diaspora."[39] Electronically based communications maintain and even reinforce social and familial connections with the homeland.

Additionally, advances in telecommunications also enable diasporic members to cheaply and easily maintain connections with the homeland. For example, in the United States, a startup telecommunications company in California is now offering free international long-distance calling to over 50 nations by dialing a phone number in Iowa and following simple prompts.[40] If one has even a low cost cell phone service that offers free nights and weekend calls, then anyone can call home overseas everyday, for free. Ironically, the 50 nations available for free dialing are among some of the biggest contributors of diasporas (and immigrants, as a whole) to the United States, including China, Mexico, Hong Kong, Ireland, and South Korea, among others.[41] These new and improved electronic forms of communication reinforce the critical diasporic ties to the homeland because the cost, both real and social, of e-mail, cell phones, faxes, and web sites are so low.[42] The inexpensive reinforcement of ties to the homeland makes complicates the host nation's problem of assimilation by making it easier to maintain the ties to the homeland.

TRANSPORTATION BARRIER

Another traditional barrier to migration and diaspora formation was the difficulty of transportation. Initially, people migrated internationally by boat, foot, or beast of burden. All of these methods were at best unreliable, time-consuming, and expensive, and at worst, treacherous. The difficulties of transportation necessitated a surety of purpose prior to departure. However, today the tremendous advances in transport technologies make leaving the homeland to join a diaspora a simple, everyday, speedy event. Jet travel is the single biggest contributor to the

---

[39] Nonini, 565.
[40] David Hayes, "Free Overseas Calls," *Kansas City Star,* 29 October 2006, sec. D, p. 10.
[41] Future Phone Corporation, http://www.futurephone.com, last accessed 15 February 2007.
[42] Nonini, 567.

movement of peoples around the world. The connections created by jet travel between the major cities of the world are unparalleled in world history. The heightened velocity of movement of people, goods, and capital in large part explains why contemporary groups have been able to rapidly build and sustain diasporas.[43]

The biggest advantage to diasporas brought by jet travel may not actually be the ability to cheaply move large amounts of people from the homeland to the seeded nation. Perhaps the biggest advantage can be found in the ability for the people to return home. Periodically returning to the homeland reinforces the natural ties an immigrant has left behind. It also enables the diasporic member to leave his family behind with the knowledge that he can easily return home on demand, or bring the family to visit him. Finally, low-cost, frequent jet travel enables the immigrant to conduct family and homeland visits almost at will, on short notice, without overbearing negative financial impact.

Traditionally, barriers to international migration and diaspora formation were great, if not nearly insurmountable. Communications and travel both were unreliable, expensive, and difficult. However, in modern times, these barriers are easily overcome. Thus, with advances in communication and travel technologies, diaspora formation has been able to transcend space and time limitations, and has begun to form more easily, grow quicker, and impact the seeded society in much greater terms than ever before. With the prolific growth of diasporas in the modern world, there exists myriad possible, if not probable, impacts on the receiving society.

NEGATIVE IMPACTS OF DIASPORAS

Not all of the impacts of diasporas on seeded societies are negative. For instance the cross-cultural exchange, especially in customs, traditions, goods and cuisine, from a diaspora can

---

[43] Ibid., p. 565.

be a very positive influence on a seeded society. However, this is more of a general characteristic of immigration as a whole. Without dedicated study of the negative effects of modern diasporas on seeded societies, one might easily see only at the positive or neutral impact of historic diasporas. Indeed, in the past, the diasporas of the Old World, the Phoenicians, the Greeks, the Jews, the Armenians, were simply protected traders and sojourners. In the Ottoman empire, diasporas constituted set-apart religious communities, dhimmis, physically and economically protected but largely unimportant to the seeded societies. In Europe, the Jews were largely confined to urban ghettos and at the mercy of autocratic and anti-Semitic regimes, and thus marginalized. Even today, diasporic Palestinians in the Gulf States have little to no citizenship rights and have little impact on the seeded countries. However, in the free, open, affluent, western societies of the modern day, there has been a dramatic change in the civic, political, and especially economic impact of many diasporas.[44]

Diasporas in modern times can affect a seeded country in many ways which tend to have a largely negative effect. While several of the negative effects of diasporas will be discussed here, the list will be by no means exhaustive. The negative effects discussed will be used as a building block for Chapter 5, where a discussion of how to mitigate the negative effects of diaspora within the United States will be undertaken.

BREAKDOWN OF NATION-STATES

The Treaty of Westphalia in 1648 ended the 30 Years War within Europe. More importantly, however, was the lasting effect it would have on international politics from its signing to present day. The Westphalia peace treaty is largely credited with establishing the modern international system of nation-states in which all countries are equal, sovereign and

---

[44] Pnina Werbner, "Chaordic Diasporas", see Ember, ed., 549.

should live free from external intervention. This was the beginning of the western tendency to draw borders on a map where no such borders previously existed.[45] For nearly 300 years, it has been the nation-state that has been the major actor on the international scene. This trend has begun to turn towards globalization in the last 50 years as the world heads towards more connectivity and interdependence through a globalized economy. As global trade has become a more and more dominant factor, humans have naturally migrated to seek a better life. However, even though people are migrating to seek a better life, one of the characteristics of a diaspora is that the people of a diaspora tend to maintain ties to the homeland, and even long for an eventual return.

The declining costs of migration for those who replanted their roots in nations in which they had connections based on previous flow of family and friends has given rise to modern day diasporas. Additionally, this explains the strong clustering effect of international migration, with people from the same country ending up together in another country halfway around the world.[46] Sending societies often encourage diasporic political participation; while most Western seeded societies seem to tolerate dual citizenship and transnational activism as never before.[47] The diasporas are forming advocacy networks and proliferating with the goal of changing the behavior of states, whether it is the behavior of the seeded state or the homeland.[48]

Because of the increased activism, diasporas are increasingly challenging the idea of the nation-state both in the seeded societies and in the sending societies. Chinese-Americans protest against human right violations in China, and Cuban-Americans against the Communist regime of Castro. Grenadians, Haitians, and Filipinos based in New York City diasporas have lobbied

---

[45] William Easterly, *The White Man's Burden* (New York: The Penguin Press, 2005), 293.
[46] John F. Helliwell, *How Much Do National Borders Matter?* (Washington, D.C.: Brookings Institute Press, 1998), 80.
[47] Werbner, 544.

(some would say successfully) for intervention in their respective countries to remove hated authoritarian regimes. These examples show the increasing influence of diasporas, especially in the west, as they grow larger and begin to hold political sway. Diaspora members are, in fact, engaging in "long distance nationalism" without worrying about accountability to the governments they oppose.[49]

This long distance nationalism has been enabled by the development of global media and communication technologies and poses a very real and present danger to the international system of nation-states and the idea of non-interference. The United States and most of its partners and allies rely on the international system to further their goals around the world and provide security and stability for their citizens. In fact, the United Nations, the current world government body, is founded upon the ideas descended from the Peace of Westphalia. It appears that the ideas of sovereignty, non-interference, and world order can be undermined simply by the seeding of diasporas, without a shot being fired in anger. If this is so, then it is time for the United States to begin taking diasporic issues seriously and looking to find ways to mitigate this negative effect.

INFLUENCE FROM EXILE

A related issue to influencing the governmental actions of the seeded nations is the ability of diasporic members to influence governmental and population actions of the homeland from abroad. This phenomenon is labeled by diaspora expert Nicholas Van Hear as "influence from exile."[50] The amount of influence depends directly on the amount of resources that the diaspora can mobilize, and this, in turn, is directly related to the physical location of the diaspora. Obviously, the resources that can be generated in Western nations greatly exceed that which can

---

[48] Margaret Keck and Kathryn Sikkink, *Activists Beyond Borders* (Ithaca, NY: Cornell University Press, 1998), 39.
[49] Werbner., 544.
[50] Nicholas Van Hear, "Refugee Diasporas or Refugees in Diaspora", see Ember, ed., 585.

be generated in non-Western nations. The vast majority of influence arrives in the form of remittances. Remittances, defined similarly in many sources, but best defined by the Visa Corporation, are payments sent to beneficiaries through formal channels such as financial institutions and other regulated agencies, or through informal channels such as cash couriers and local merchants.[51]

In a recent report from the World Bank's Migration and Remittances Team, recorded remittances sent home by migrants from developing countries are expected to reach $199 billion in 2006, up from $188 billion in 2005, and more than double the level in 2001. Worldwide flows of remittances, including those to high-income countries, are estimated to have to grown to $268 billion in 2006. This amount, however, reflects only transfers through official channels. Econometric analysis and available household surveys suggest that unrecorded flows through informal channels may add 50% or more to recorded flows. Including these unrecorded flows, the true size of remittances is larger than foreign direct investment flows and more than twice as large as official aid received by developing countries. Remittances are the largest source of external financing in many developing countries.[52]

Two note-worthy facts stand out in this report. First, the current amount of remittance does not include unrecorded remittances, which, while difficult to measure, may add 50% to recorded flows. Which nation is, by far, the largest single source of remittance outflow in the world? The United States.[53] This is evidence that the United States is the destination of choice for diaspora formation. Secondly, remittances far exceed that of official aid. This is again a less than desirable situation for the United States. Part of the United States national identity is that of

---

[51] Visa Corporation, "Visa Remittance Solutions", http://corporate.visa.com/pd/pdf/remittance.pdf, last accessed 15 February 2007.
[52] World Bank, "Remittance Trends 2006", http://siteresources.worldbank.org/NEWS/MiscContent/21124588/mad.pdf, last accessed 15 February 2007.

charity and giving. As such, the United States is the largest donor of official development assistance in the world. In fact, Figure 3 shows, in 2005, the United States gave more than twice amount of its nearest competitor, Japan.[54]

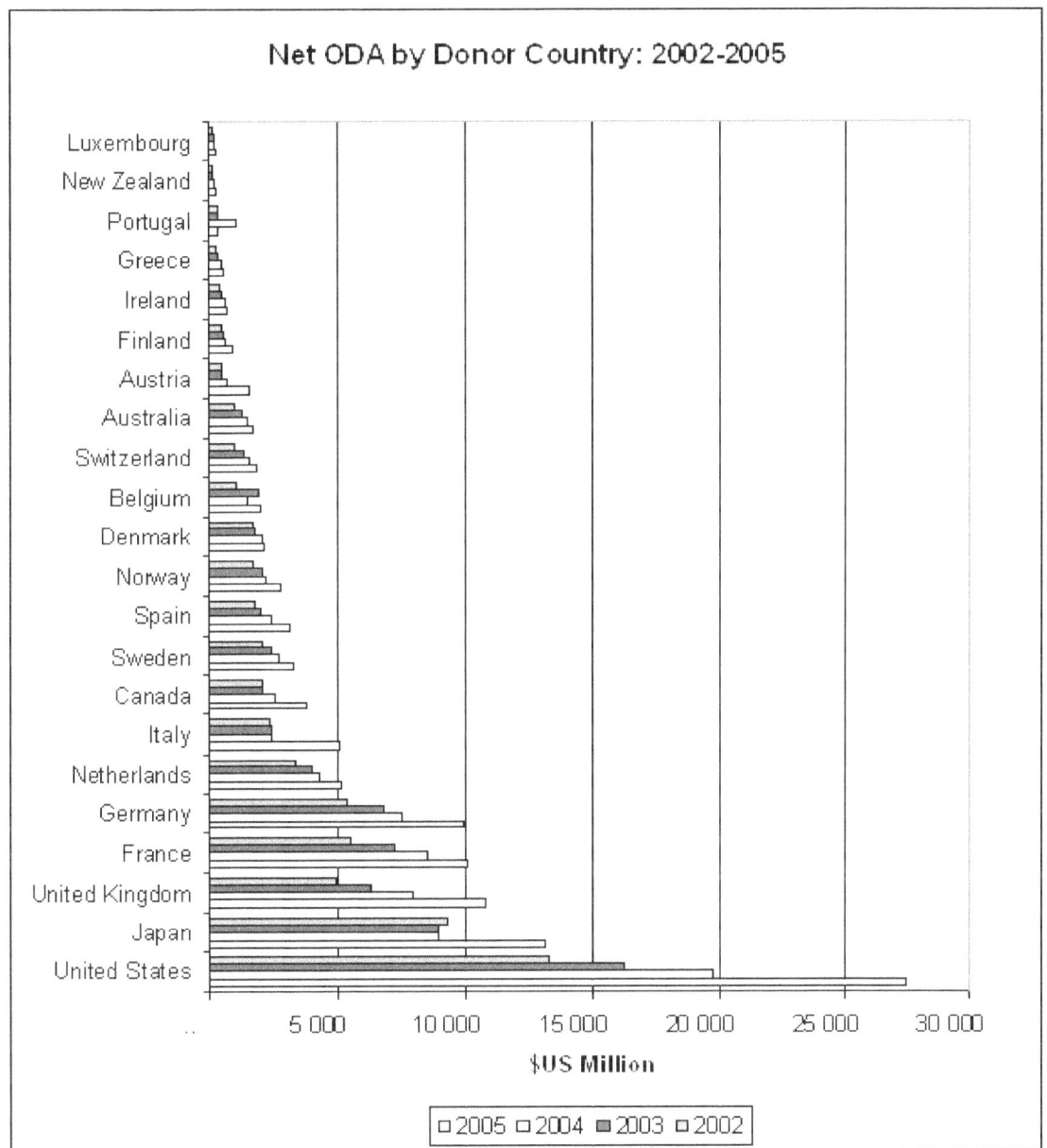

Figure 3 - Net ODA by Donor Country: 2002-2005

[53] Ibid.

Neglecting the other G8 states of Japan, United Kingdom, France, Germany, Italy, Canada, and Russia, the United States gave over five times the amount of the next largest donor country. However, the amount of remittances flowing out of the United States by migrant workers far exceeds the generosity of the United States government. For example, remittance flow to Latin America alone this year is expected to exceed $45 Billion[55], over 50% more than the total ODA from the US government to the rest of the world. If part of the United States' strategy of influencing other nations is to provide international aid, and if the amount of influence can be directly related to dollar amount of aid, the United States government is simply not keeping up with dollar totals by diasporic remittances, and can expect to have diminishing diplomatic and economic influence over developing nations. Figure 4 below shows how US ODA has grown over the past 6 years. [56] But this simply is not enough to keep up with remittances.

---

[54] Organization for Economic Co-operation and Development, http://www.oecd.org/countrylist, last accessed 14 February 2007.

[55] Matt Whitaker, "Immigrants Send Billions Abroad Each Year", November 14, 2006. Apostille US, http://apostille.us/news/ immigrants_send_billions_abroad_each_year_now_banks_want_a _piece_of_the_action.shtml.

[56] Department of State website http://www.state.gov/r/pa/prs/ps/2006/66060.htm.

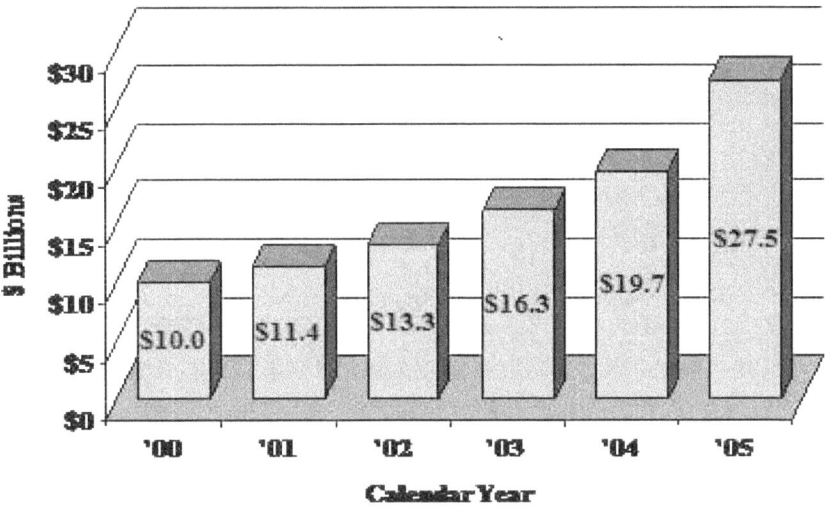

Figure 4 - Net U.S. Official Development Assistance

Remittances can have a positive influence on the diasporic homeland. For example, remittances from the diaspora help individuals and families to survive during conflict and to sustain communities in times of crisis such as economic depression or famine. Much of the remittances are used in the homeland for daily subsistence needs, health care, or housing. However, it is the negative side of remittances that is of concern. The negative effects of diasporic remittances become immediately apparent with a cursory examination of what other uses remittances might serve.

First, diasporic remittances do not go to the homeland government, instead they are sent directly to the population at large. ODA from the United States, however, goes directly to foreign governments for them to use as they please, with some stipulations. This can cause an immediate conflict of interest for the United States. For instance, the United States could be funding or supporting a legitimate government which happens to be in a battle against insurgency occurring within that nation. Meanwhile, remittances and other transfers from diasporic members within the United States could very well be going to help the insurgency, thereby perpetuating the conflict.

Secondly, because of the wealth available in the United States and its relatively open doors to migrants, Paul Collier, Director of the Development Research Group of the World Bank, has concluded "[i]f a country has recently had a civil war…and has a very large diaspora in the United States…its chances of [future] conflict are 36%. If it has an unusually small diaspora [in the United States] its chances of conflict are only 6%."[57] Mr. Collier does not give the source of his statistics and, therefore, one has a difficult time concluding that large diasporas necessarily cause post-civil war conflict to increase by a factor of six. However, there does seem to be some logic in his claim. This is especially true if one considers a further statement by Mr. Collier later in his report:

> "Diasporas sometimes harbour rather romanticized attachments to their group of origin and may nurse grievances as a form of asserting continued belonging. They are much richer than the people in their country of origin and so can afford to finance vengeance. Above all, they do not have to suffer any of the awful consequences of renewed conflict because they are not living in the country. Hence, they are a ready market for rebel groups touting vengeance and so are a source of finance for renewed conflict."[58]

The "romanticized attachment" Mr. Collier refers to is a previously cited and well-recognized characteristic of diasporas, and the support of the diaspora to the homeland certainly seems to be plausible given the types of diasporas described earlier by Robin Cohen. The influence from exile in regards to the monetary amount that can be sent to the homeland from a diaspora can serve to be destabilizing in the homeland and work counter to the national interests of the United States. The negative effect of remittances has been clearly shown to have influence and diplomatic consequences on both the homeland and the seeded nation. However, perhaps the greatest future negative effect of diasporas on the seeded nation can be found in the drain on the economy of the seeded nation.

---

[57] Paul Collier, "Economic Causes of Civil Conflict and Their Implications for Policy", World Bank, http://www.worldbank.org/research/conflict/papers/civilconflict.pdf, last accessed 15 February 2007.

THE MONEY DRAIN

The money drain of a diaspora on the seeded nation can be broadly divided into two categories: the exportation of the host nation gross domestic product (GDP), and additional strain on public welfare systems by diaspora members. Together, these two categories combine for a potent one-two punch to the economy of the host nation. The economics of immigration have long been studied, especially the negative effects on the economy. Dr. Jenks, again writing as long ago as 1926, says, "It can hardly be said that taken by itself the sending back to the old country of the savings of the immigrant is directly an injury to the United States."[59] Even more contemporary authors agree with Jenks' assessment: "...immigration...is making us poorer, not richer," said then-Governor Richard Lamm of Colorado.[60] However, looking objectively at the effects of diasporas requires more specific observations than "poorer" or "injurious". More analysis is required to decide if diasporas truly have negative effects on the United States economy.

A nation's GDP, generally speaking, is a well-known and widely-accepted view of a nation's wealth. Figure 5 shows the world's nations in relation to their GDP in terms of millions of US dollars. A cursory look at Figure 5 appears to show several countries, including China, France, Germany, the United Kingdom, and Japan on par with the United States in the "above $2 trillion category".[61]

---

[58] Ibid., 14.

[59] Jenks, 16.

[60] Steven Anzovin, ed., *The Problem of Immigration* (New York: The H. Wilson Company, 1985), 11.

[61] "International Monetary Fund graphic", http://www.imf.org/external/ pubs/ft/weo/2006/01/data/dbcoutm.cfm, last accessed 15 January 2007.

Figure 5 - World Gross Domestic Product

In reality, the United States, with a nation of only 300 million people, has far and away the largest GDP on the planet. Graphical depictions such as Figure 5 often belie what is really occurring. This is one of the problems of trying to understand the negative effects of diaspora remittance. On the other hand, Table 2 clearly shows the monstrous GDP of the United States when compared to the rest of the world's top ten GDP nations. In fact, estimated figures for 2006 show that the US GDP is triple that of its nearest competitor, Japan.[62] Only the combined nations of the European Union exceed the GDP of the United States.

Table 2 - World GDP

Country	2000	2001	2002	2003	2004	2005	2006	2007
World	31649.8	31455.91	32714.12	36750.96	41258.03	44454.843	**47766.580**	51056.588
EU	8389.92	8475.822	9269.138	11273.138	12980.129	13502.800	**14205.938**	15338.404
US	9816.97	10127.950	10469.600	10960.750	11712.475	12455.825	**13262.074**	13928.462

---

[62] "International Monetary Fund GDP Statistics", http://www.imf.org/external/pubs/ft/weo/2006/02/data/index.aspx, last accessed 14 February 2007.

Japan	4650.94	4090.194	3911.581	4237.073	4587.146	4567.441	**4463.590**	4599.358
Germany	1905.79	1892.595	2024.060	2444.284	2744.221	2791.737	**2890.092**	3036.853
China	1198.48	1324.812	1453.837	1640.966	1931.642	2234.133	**2554.200**	2871.019
UK	1445.19	1435.626	1574.470	1814.638	2155.162	2229.472	**2357.580**	2552.655
France	1333.00	1341.428	1463.901	1805.028	2059.716	2126.719	**2227.330**	2370.843
Italy	1100.56	1118.318	1223.236	1510.056	1726.788	1765.537	**1841.042**	1949.878
Canada	725.158	715.632	734.773	868.485	993.908	1132.436	**1273.144**	1357.073
Spain	582.377	608.882	688.501	882.667	1041.038	1126.565	**1216.736**	1325.252
Russia	259.702	306.583	345.486	431.429	589.025	763.287	**975.338**	1158.921

Historically, an enormous GDP has been one of the sources of power for the United States. At first glance it appears as though it remains an advantage today. However, looking at the trend of the GDP of the United States as a percentage world's GDP reveals a declining trend. For instance, in 2000, the US' GDP constituted fully 30% of the world's total. That number has declined to 27% this year and is projected to decline further next year. Meanwhile, as mentioned earlier, remittances out of the United States and into other nations are exploding. If one accepts the numbers from the World Bank and other sources, remittances worldwide are growing anywhere between 25%-30% per year, with those from the United States growing even faster. By comparison, the United States GDP is only growing at an annual rate of 2-3%. While $60 billion in remittances currently do not have a significant impact on total GDP, at some point in the not too distant future, remittances will begin to significantly impact US GDP as remittances double, conservatively, every 5 years and GDP increases only 15% over the same 5 year period. This is of great concern to the United States.

There are at least two reasons for concern. First of all, the United States relies on its economy as one of its elements of national power. As the US GDP is exported to other countries, their GDP is increased without any effort on their part. This naturally closes the gap between the US and others. Additionally, there is evidence to suggest that a dollar leaving the country in remittance actually has more than a dollar's worth of negative effect on the US GDP. Speaking broadly, for every dollar sent abroad, more than a dollar's worth of productive labor has been expended in the US. The worker has fully earned his dollar. However, if that dollar, instead of being sent to the home country, were re-invested in the United States, then the benefit would be greater. For example, America would receive the benefit of the labor plus the dollar re-invested in either goods or savings within the United States.[63] If one accepts the logic of this line of argument, then the negative effect of a dollar of exported GDP is actually compounded.

The second broad category within the "money drain" is the strain on public services and welfare systems due to the presence of the diasporas. Obviously, any additional population requires additional services provided by the local, state, and federal governments. This is an accepted reality of providing security and stability for the nation's populace. However, this is generally mitigated by the desire of immigrants to integrate into and become productive members of the society. Previously, this monograph has shown that this is not the case for diasporic members, resulting in additional strain on public services without the expected benefits.

States and communities provide public services largely through the raising of tax revenue by taxing goods and services. Tax-supported services such as sanitation, public transportation, education, environmental cleanup, municipal services – including fire and police protection – and a host of other related services are all utilized by people living in America simply by virtue of

---

[63] Jenks, 17.

their presence here.[64] Consequently, a diasporic member who is sending much of his earned income back to the homeland is not out in the community purchasing goods and services, generating tax revenue for the community and state. Assuming an average state and local sales tax of 8% nation-wide, the remittances of $45 billion dollars last year to Latin America removed over $3 billion dollars of tax revenue in sales tax alone. Yet diasporic members certainly were consumers and users of the public services listed above.

One economist, Donald L. Huddle of Rice University in Houston, Texas, calculated the cost of immigration to the United States in 1994 (including cost of unemployment benefits for U.S.-born workers displaced by immigrants) to be $42.5 billion more than the immigrants paid in taxes.[65] While this number includes all immigration, not just diasporic immigration, it is still a staggering number. The lost tax revenue and the added strain on public health and welfare services is, without question, a negative contribution to the society, and perpetuates the negative effect of the money drain created by diaspora existence.

DANGER IN OUR MIDST

It is at our own peril to ignore the possible negative consequences of diaspora formation within the United States. In an increasingly globalized economy where fates of nations rely more and more on economic power rather that military power, it is imperative for the United States to retain its economic advantages in order to maintain its place as the lone superpower. Other nations will challenge the United States economically and militarily eventually, however, the United States must recognize the ways in which diasporas in the United States are aiding its competitors. Robin Cohen sums up the potential negative consequences like this: "…the general point is that many immigrants are no longer individualized or obedient prospective citizens.

---

[64] Georges Fauriol, "US Immigration Policy and the National Interest", see Anzovin, ed., 110.
[65] Scott Barbour, ed., *Immigration Policy* (San Diego: Greenhaven Press, Inc., 1995), 8.

Instead, they may retain dual citizenship, agitate for special trade deals with their homelands, demand aid in exchange for electoral support and seek to influence social and foreign policy."[66]

---

[66] Cohen, 194.

CHAPTER 4

The United States is undoubtedly a nation of immigrants. As referenced in Chapter 1, over 99% of the US population was born in a foreign land or are descendants of those from a foreign land. In the modern world, barriers to migration have been lowered and the ability to communicate and stay connected with the homeland has made immigration easier and easier. Increasingly, the United States is the destination of choice for migrants. The "Great Melting Pot", however, is being replaced largely by insoluble ingredients that refuse to mix with the other ingredients. Diasporas are becoming more and more common in the United States. This chapter will look briefly at diaspora formation within the United States.

CURRENT DIASPORA ROUTES

Globalization, the idea most popularly espoused by Thomas Friedman, is generally accepted to mean the process of growing interconnection between previously separated human populations on a global scale, often associated with the last several centuries of modernity.[67] The ability of people to move quickly, cheaply, and easily around the world and back has aided diasporic formation in more and more formalized ways. But where are the diasporas forming and from where are they originating? Donald Nonini answers that question in an article on diasporas (emphasis added):[68]

> The major routes and itineraries of [modern] diasporic migrations can be readily summarized as follows:
> • Diasporas of ethnic groups originally residing in post-socialist Eastern Europe and Eurasia to Europe, *the United States* and the Gulf States (e.g., Russians, Chechens, Rumanians, Bulgarians).
> • Diasporas of ethnic groups residing in northern and central Africa and the Mediterranean to Western Europe (e.g., Algerians, Moroccans, Senegalese, Turks).

---

[67] Nonini (2005), 564.
[68] Ibid., 566.

- Diasporas of ethnic groups originally residing in the Caribbean to the United Kingdom, Western Europe, and *the United States* (e.g., Jamaicans, Dominicans, Haitians, Puerto Ricans).
- Diasporas of ethnic groups residing in South Asia to the United Kingdom, *the United States*, the Gulf States, and urban Southeast Asia (e.g., Pakistanis, Indians, Bangladeshis, Nepalese).
- Diasporas of ethnic groups residing in peripheral nation-states in Southeast Asia to more affluent nations-states of Southeast Asia, the Gulf States and *the United States* (e.g., Filipinos, Burmese).
- Diasporas of ethnic groups residing in Central and South America to *the United States* (e.g., Mexicans, Guatemalans, Colombians, Ecuadorians).

The United States appears in five of the six major diaspora routes identified by Nonini. His use of the words "readily identified" leaves no doubt as to the United States being the number one destination for diaspora formation. But why choose the United States? Who is forming diasporas within the United States? What makes it an attractive destination for diaspora formation? The following sections attempt to shed some light on the answers to these questions.

STILL THE GOLDEN DOOR[69]

If Donald Nonini's diasporic routes are to be taken at face value, then the United States is clearly the destination of choice for diasporas. The economic advantages of the capitalistic system in the United States are apparent and were discussed in the previous chapter. However, economic advantages are not sufficient to explain why the United States is the number one choice for diasporas. For example, if the United States populace was hostile to foreigners, or if the government stopped allowing immigrants in the door, then diaspora formation would be more difficult and/or less desirable. This section will examine some of the reasons, besides its economy, why the United States is susceptible to diaspora formation. Heading the list of reasons why America is the target of diaspora formation is: lax immigration laws, unenforceable

---

[69] David M. Reimers, *Still the Golden Door* (New York: Columbia University Press, 1992), ix.

immigration statutes, a long, unfortified border, and the presence of many so-called "global cities", relative to other nations.

POROUS BORDER

Borders serve a variety of functions – political, psychological, and cultural. In their most basic sense, they demarcate the boundary between here and there. In doing so, they determine between members of one nation and those of another. In addition, borders in the international nation-state system are necessary for countries to carry on the form of government its people have chosen. The United States is no exception to this construct.[70] Saskia Sassen, a professor of urban planning at Columbia University, claims "borders no longer are sites for imposing levies. Rather, they are transmitting membranes guaranteeing the free flow of goods, capital, and information."[71]

The United States has borders with only two other nations, Mexico and Canada, both of whom have, in modern times been friendly neighbors in an official capacity. The US border with Canada, while longer than that with Mexico, is widely accepted to be fairly secure and not crossed nearly as much by legal or illegal immigrants as the southern border is. The US-Canada border is not currently a significant contributor to US immigration, and by extension, to diaspora formation.

However, the Mexico-US border is a different story. Figure 6 is a depiction of the Mexico-US border.[72] The border is 1,952 miles long with only 21 official crossing sites, and is the most frequently crossed border in the world with over 350,000,000 people crossing legally

---

[70] Stanley A. Renshon, *The 50% American* (Washington D.C.: Georgetown University Press, 2005), 130.
[71] Saskia Sassen, "Immigration Policy Should Reflect Economic Globalization", see Barbour, ed., 68.
[72] Federal Motor Carrier Safety Administration, http://www.fmcsa.dot.gov/images/us-mexico-border.jpg, last accessed 15 February 2007.

each year.[73] While there are border patrols on either side of the border and fences in some

popular crossing areas, the border is largely un-patrolled and un-enforced. Although this may be

changing in the wake of the September 11, 2001, terrorist attacks and recent concerns over illegal

immigration, the US border with Mexico remains largely demilitarized and porous. This "un-

enforced border with Mexico is an un-enforced border with the world."[74] Besides allowing many

illegal immigrants into the US every year, the porous border also allows legal immigrants to enter

the US easily and return home with little to no effort or cost. Mexican immigration laws are also

more lax than that of the United States, which means if one can get into Mexico, then one can get

into the United States.

Figure 6 - United States - Mexico Border

[73] US Embassy in Mexico, "Borders and Law Enforcement,
http://mexico.usembassy.gov/mexico/eborder_mechs.html, last accessed 15 February 2007.

GLOBAL CITIES

Some cities in the world have become so important in the world scene strategically, culturally, politically, and financially as to be known as "global cities". The concept of global cities is largely credited to Saskia Sassen in her book, *The Global City*, written in 1991. She defines "global cities" as cities that have become so strategically important in the world system as to denationalize time and space. In other words, the global age of transportation and digits has enabled some cities to become something larger than the nation in which they happen to lie. Since then, the idea of global cities has been examined, discussed, debated, modified, and codified so much that it is difficult to nail down exactly what a global city is. However, some characteristics do seem to be common among most of the definitions offered. Among these characteristics are large populations, significant financial capacity, first-rate transportation capabilities, presence of high-technology, and centers of tourism. In the West, the presence of large immigrant communities, such as Chinatowns and Little Italy's, is also a chief characteristic. As noted before, it is difficult to find two lists of criteria of global cities that match. But one thing is clear: many cities in the United States dominate all of the lists. Figure 7 provides a representative example of global cities presented by the Globalization and World Studies Group and Network (GaWC).[75] One quickly sees the United States has three of the top ten leading world cities and 11 of the top 55.

---

[74] Georges Fauriol, "US Immigration Policy and the National Interest", *The Humanist,* May/June 1984, see Anzovin, ed., 113.

[75] Globalization and World Cities, "The World According to GAWC", http://www.lboro.ac.uk/gawc/citymap.html, last accessed 15 February 2007.

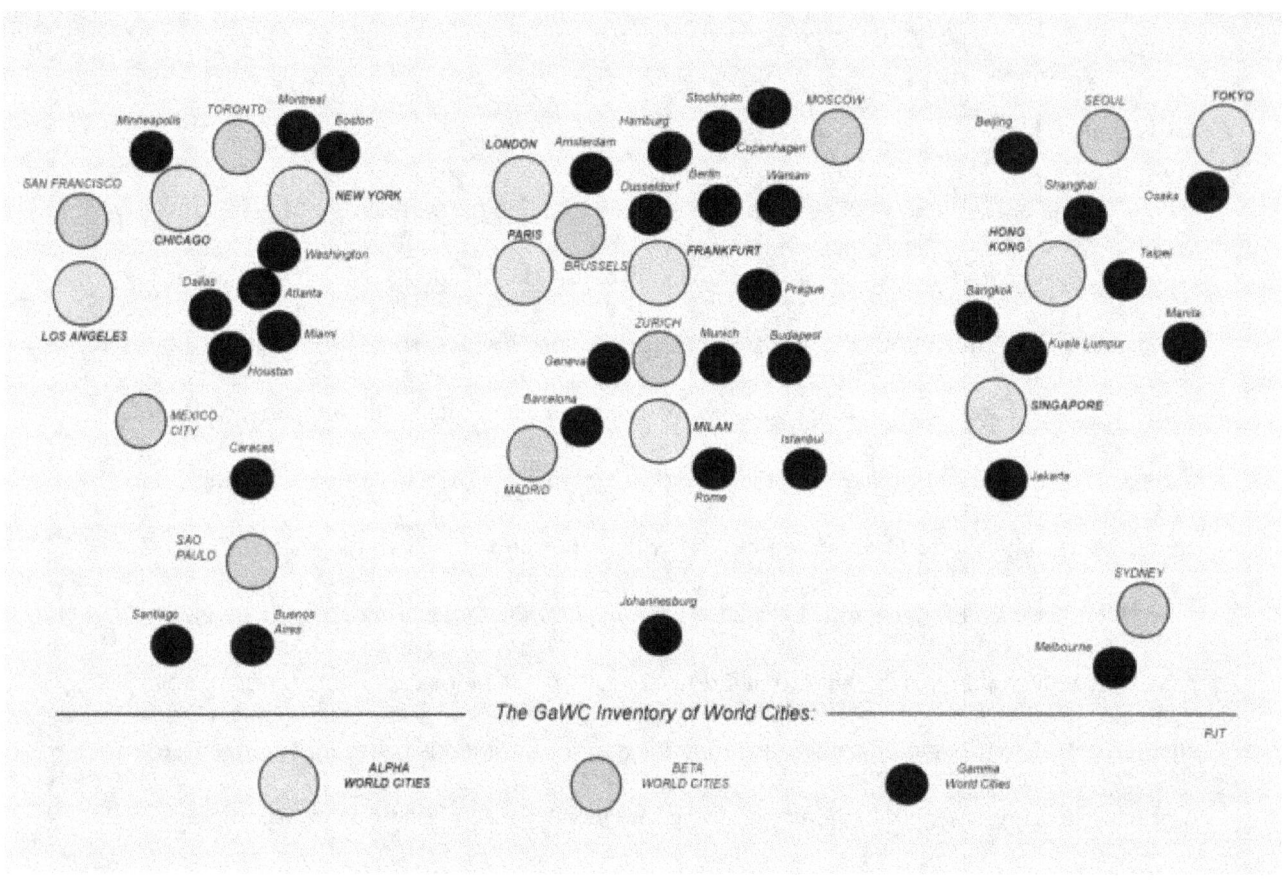

Figure 7 - World Cities

Within the global cities, international migration of a particular kind develops. Citizens of other countries arrive to fill jobs across the spectrum of skills from professionals and mangers to entertainers, waiters, and even prostitutes; many with no intent to remain permanently. The global cities are connected by ever-increasing methods of transportation and communication. This allows the members of a diaspora to be, almost by definition, more mobile than people who are rooted in national spaces. In the age of globalization, diaspora members find themselves competitive in the international labor market – "after all, waiters or prostitutes who can address international customers in their own languages are likely to have a distinct edge over their competitors."[76] With cities growing ever more international in flavor every day, the opportunity increases for citizens of a foreign nation to migrate, form a diaspora, and never fully integrate into the society in which they have moved. The ability to conduct business in their native tongue and live in smaller versions of their homelands transplanted to a new country makes it even easier to remain tied to their homeland.

UNENFORCABLE LAX IMMIGRATION LAWS

The United States, indeed the entire Western Hemisphere, has been peopled by immigrants. During the Colonial period, most US immigrants came from Europe, mostly Britain, France, Scandinavia and the Netherlands, in addition to the nearly 500,000 Africans brought in as slaves. Immigrants really poured into the nation after the Revolutionary War. The Founding Fathers worried that immigrants from lands with different political beliefs might undermine the fledgling democracy, but the need for more people to drive the economy and carry out westward expansion outweighed such concerns.[77]

A specific policy covering immigration did not really begin to emerge until the 20th Century. By then, the people of the United States, and the rest of the world, had become accustomed to little or no restrictions on entering the Melting Pot. In 1875, the Supreme Court of the US struck down all state laws attempting to restrict immigration, effectively leaving the job of immigration to the US Congress.[78] A hodge-podge of exclusionary regulation, especially against Chinese, and citizenship requirements, such as the ability to read and write English, highlighted an ineffectual attempt by Congress to keep certain immigrants out and to let others in during the first part of the 20th Century. This all changed with the end of World War I and the rise of

---

[76] Cohen, 168-169.
[77] Unatributed, "Immigration Policy: A Historical Overview", *The CQ Researcher*, September 24, 1993, see Barbour, ed., 11.
[78] Martin v. Wilkes, United States Supreme Court, 1875.

isolationism in the United States. Congress passed the 1921 Quota Act which limited the number of new immigrants for the first time, and attempted to maintain the current ethnic and cultural mix in the United States by limiting the number of admissible immigrants of a given nationality at 3% of the amount already in the United States. As a result, immigration plummeted in the 1930's, only to rise again with the onset of WWII.

Beginning in 1942, foreigners were permitted to enter the United States temporarily for work in order to alleviate worker shortages created by the draft. Most of these workers came from Mexico, harvested crops, sent the money back to Mexico, and then returned.[79] This was the beginning of the end for exclusions and quotas. By 1965, the civil rights movement gained such momentum that all restrictions based on national origins were lifted. The winning of the Cold War solidified the United States' position as the most desirable place to live and prosper. The 1990's saw the largest amount of immigrant flows into the United States in its history. Immigration has been on the rise ever since, aided by legislation such as the 1990 Immigration Act which actually increased the amount of immigrants allowed into the United States each year.[80]

A largely ineffectual buffet of immigration legislation passed by Congress containing little to no consistent guidelines for immigration allowed people of all nations to enter the United States with very little difficulty. Immigration policy swayed in the political wind of the day until the United States was left with an unchecked immigrant flow from all over the world. Immigration numbers were so large as to overwhelm any effective enforcement of inflows or allow for effective enforcement of legislation across the nation. The current immigration policy status quo has been slowly overwhelmed by events and forces that are prompting cries of alarm.[81]

---

[79] Barbour, ed., 14.
[80] Ibid., 15.
[81] Fauriol, see Anzovin, ed., 115.

DIASPORAS INSIDE THE UNITED STATES

While there are no official records kept by the United States government concerning diaspora formation and who is comprising them, general demographic, immigration and remittance statistics can aid the process of identifying diasporas within the United States. For instance, the proportion of Americans who were born in another country is growing rapidly as immigrants flood to the United States. In 2000, nearly one in nine Americans was foreign born, up from one in 20 only 30 years before. The 51% majority of foreign-born residents counted by the 2000 census arrived from Latin America. Another 26% came from Asia, but only 16% came from Europe. Contrast these statistics with the 1960 census when the leading countries of foreign-born citizens in the United States were, in order, from Italy, Germany, Canada, the United Kingdom, and Poland.[82]

A good place to start looking for locations of diasporas within the United States is to take a look at Figure 7. Ten of the eleven cities listed (all except Minneapolis) make up 10 of the top 11 urban areas found within the United States, and also rank within the top 70 cities globally. The global city of Miami illustrates perfectly the idea of diasporas within the United States. Miami has the highest proportion of foreign-born residents of any major metropolitan area in the United States, proportionally 50% more than either Los Angeles or New York. According to the 2000 United States census figures, 50% of Miami-Dade County's residents are foreign born. When the second generation is added, the percentage comes to over 70%. Of the foreign-born population, 87% are from the America's. The assortment of diasporic communities can be observed in the numbers of "Little" communities found in Miami. Little Haiti is just south of the downtown, Little Havana is in central Miami, and Little Managua is west near the Everglades.

---

[82] Cheryl Russell, *Demographics of the United States* (Ithaca, New York: New Strategist Publications, 2003), 318.

47

There are even claims of Little Lima, Little Rio, and Little Buenos Aires.[83] The immigrants are grouping together into like-communities outside the mainstream American society. On the other hand, with the numbers of foreign born persons in Miami and their little communities, the diasporas may be transforming the mainstream American society in South Florida.

Los Angeles is another example of diaspora growth within the United States. It also happens to be one of places where the Latino and Asian diasporas co-exist. During the 1990's, about 4 million new immigrants were added to the population of California, 41% of them settling in Los Angeles and another 9% of them in nearby Orange County. At mid-decade, more than half a million students were considered limited English proficiency.[84] The US Census Bureau reported in 2005 that the population of 10 million persons Los Angeles County was made up of 46.5% Latino and 13% Asian.[85]

There is ample evidence that the Latino and Asian populations are forming diasporas and the state government is only exacerbating the situation. First of all, there are over 83 languages spoken in Los Angeles County, and the schools are the most affected. At Hollywood High alone, there are 60 languages spoken in students' homes. Instead of requiring all to speak English, the state instead has required that a school form a bilingual class when 20 or more students speak a foreign language as their first language.[86] This is allowing students to maintain their native tongues at the expense of the state and provides no impetus to integrate into a country that is widely recognized as English-speaking. In many cases "whole villages from Mexico have

---

[83] Lisa N. Konczal, "Miami Diasporas", see Ember, ed., 524.
[84] William A.V. Clark, "Immigration and California Communities", February 1999, Center for Immigration Studies, http://www.cis.org/articles/1999/back299.html, last accessed 15 February 2007.
[85] US Census Bureau, "State and Country Quick Facts", http://quickfacts.census.gov/qfd/states/06/06037.html, last accessed 15 February 2007.
[86] Laurel Leff, "The Los Angeles Melting Pot", *Immigrants, Refugees, and U.S. Policy* (New York: The H.W. Wilson Company, 1981) Grant S. McClellan, ed., 107.

slowly, and sometimes not so slowly, have transported themselves from Mexico to Southern California, where they have recreated…their homeland."[87]

While the over 1 million Asian residents pales in size when compared to the 4.5 million Latinos, the Asians do represent a sizeable portion of the population in Los Angeles county. Koreans, Vietnamese, and Chinese (both mainland and Taiwanese) make up the vast majority of Asian immigrants in Los Angeles. As early as 1988, Los Angeles was dubbed by John Schwartz, a *Newsweek* writer, as the "Eastern Capital of Asia."[88] Mr. Schwartz notes that one could visit China, Vietnam, the Philippines, Thailand, Vietnam, and Japan, all on one tank of gas. The profound economic impact of Asian influence is evidenced by the fact that three-quarters of the office space in downtown Los Angeles is foreign owned, a third of it by the Japanese.[89]

The Asian immigrants have settled, like the Latinos in Miami, in enclaves and created smaller versions of their homelands. The Koreans, which number over 200,000, have created a "Koreatown" with over 6000 businesses and the majority of the Korean immigrants.[90] Chinatowns are growing fast as well. Author Timothy Fong cites the existence of six discernible Chinatowns in Los Angeles County. Five of the Chinatowns lie outside the city limits and are not tourist attractions like the main Chinatown downtown.[91] These suburban Chinatowns are thought to be the first of their kind in the United States. While the suburban location of Chinatowns could suggest intent to remain permanently in the United States, the fact that the Chinese are remaining in enclaves and maintaining a strong Chinese connection does suggest continued diaspora formation.

---

[87] Clark, http://www.cis.org/articles/1999/back299.html, last accessed 15 February 2007.

[88] John Schwartz, "The Eastern Capital of Asia", *Immigration to the United States* (New York: H.W. Wilson Company, 1992), edited by Robert Emmet Long, 108.

[89] Ibid, 110.

[90] Leff, 109.

[91] Timothy P. Fong, *The First Suburban Chinatown* (Philadelphia: Temple University Press, 1994), 14.

The cities of Miami and Los Angeles offer strong evidence of diaspora formation and propagation in the nation's largest cities. However diasporas are not limited to the currently recognized global cities. America has run out of frontiers. Immigrants are seeking work outside the large cities and coastal areas, work that will provide them with enough income to subsist in the United States and send remittances back to the homeland to support their family left behind. On 8 December 2006, a quick Google search for "diasporas in the United States" returned results about Irish, Vietnamese, Armenian, Chinese, Korean, African, Haitian, Indian, Latino, Mexican, and Afghan diasporas, all within the first 20 listings. Diaspora growth is a reality, especially within the United States. Countries such as Israel, Armenia, and others even have governmental offices devoted to the development of diasporas abroad. Now that the existence of diasporas and the potential threats from their existence have been identified, Chapter 5 offers some ideas on how to mitigate the negative impacts of diasporas upon the United States.

CHAPTER 5

MITIGATING THE EFFECTS

In today's complex world environment, the definition of power seems to be changing as quickly as the newest computer or flat-screen television. Military power, as a form of influence, is on the decrease, and economic and diplomatic power is on the increase. Economic power comes in many forms, but a generally accepted way of measuring that power and comparing it with others is the Gross Domestic Product. Diplomatic power also comes in many forms but can largely be viewed as the sway a country holds in the international nation-state system and the decisions a nation makes when dealing with those states. It has been demonstrated that diasporas can have a negative effect on America's on the economic and diplomatic instruments of national power.

If America is to maintain its place as a superpower and benefit from being the destination of choice of immigrants from all over the world, it must come to grips with the fact that the diminishing influence of military power leaves the United States with the need to defend, if not increase, its diplomatic and economic elements of national power. Assuming for the foreseeable future the United States does maintain its place as the number one destination for immigrants, it must figure out ways to mitigate the negative influences of diasporas.

There exists a spectrum of options available to the United States for dealing with the negative effects of diasporas. All options revolve around immigration policy reform. Policy reform can take many forms, including the most extreme option of closing the Golden Door of entry, at least part way; to simply trying to better integrate immigrants into American society without limiting numbers of immigrants. The following suggestions are by no means the extent of available options. However, they do represent a beginning point from which to begin changing the course of current day immigration policy for the better.

POLICY REFORM

As previously cited, the United States has always had an immigration policy since it became a nation-state. In fact, the passage of naturalization laws was one of the very first acts of Congress. The problem with US immigration policy is that it has largely been inconsistent and ineffective in trying to solve identified problems. Often, Congressional partisanship gets in the way of true immigration policy reform. Even with stated limits on immigration, exemptions and other loopholes often allow ceilings to be greatly exceeded. At first glance, this should not be problematic: The United States is a large country, with plenty of open space, and only 300 million people occupying its territory. The US should easily be able to bed down as many immigrants as want to enter the nation, legally or illegally, and integrate them into American society. However, this is not the case.

More and more, immigrants are not integrating into American society. Instead, they are grouping together in large numbers at or near their points of entry into the United States and forming diasporas. Within these diasporas, the immigrants hold onto the ways of the homeland, including language, culture, and education. There is no requirement to forsake citizenship in another country to gain citizenship in the United States. The United States is the *only* country in the world to allow its citizens to do all of the following: become a citizen of one of more countries, swear allegiance to a foreign state, vote in foreign elections, run for office in another country while at the same time being a citizen in good standing of the United States, join another country's armed forces while a citizen of the United States, and fight in another country's army even if that country is hostile to the interests of the United States.[92] This is not an immigration policy; this is fuel for the flames of diaspora formation.

---

[92] Stanley A. Renshon, *The 50% American* (Washington, D.C.: Georgetown University Press, 2005), xv.

Congress must set aside its partisan views and develop an immigration policy that is consistent, fair, responsive, and shows the world that the United States is still the Golden Door of opportunity for those seeking a better life. At the same time, Congress must also ensure the safety and well-being of the American people by setting reasonable limits, controlling illegal immigration, and, above all else, ensuring the assimilation of immigrants into American societies. President George W. Bush even recognizes the Congress' role in, and the great need for, immigration reform. In his most recent State of the Union Address, the President called on Congress to "have a serious, civil, and conclusive debate, so that you [Congress] can pass and I can sign, comprehensive immigration reform into law."[93] The Golden Door of America cannot be swung wide open to allow unchecked immigration into the country. The following two sections offer suggestions on how to control the influx of immigrants, ensuring that shear numbers do not overwhelm the ability of American society to assimilate immigrants of all nationalities into the American way of life.

CLOSE THE DOOR, AT LEAST PARTWAY

Moratorium on Immigration – One way to ensure that the problem of overloading the migrant intake system and overwhelming attempts at integration is to close the Golden Door for a specified period of time. Dan Stein, the executive director of the Federation for American Immigration Reform (FAIR) based in Washington, D.C., claims, "an immigration moratorium now would provide an opportunity to examine what has happened to [American] society in the past three decades of massive, unprecedented legal and illegal immigration."[94] A temporary moratorium would offer several advantages. First, and foremost, it would allow Congress a

---

[93] President George W. Bush State of the Union Address to Combined Session of Congress, 23 January, 2007, http://www.whitehouse.gov/news/releases/2007/01/20070123-2.html, last accessed 24 January 2007.

[94] Dan Stein, "Why America Needs a Moratorium on Immigration," Barbour, ed., 22.

53

chance to study the effects of immigration and diasporas, come to some sort of consensus, and enact legislation for an effective immigration and integration policy. George F. Kennan, among others such as Stein, argues that unchecked immigration and lack of integration is a serious, even fatal, weakness in any national society.

Many authors, including Kennan, Stein, and this author, use Miami and Los Angeles as examples of the growing problem of diasporas, even though they do not use the term specifically. The idea of a moratorium is not new. In 1921, Congress enacted the Quota Act, substantially curbing immigration. The lull in immigration continued through the mid-1960's and provided the breathing space required to allow the new immigrants time to assimilate and integrate into American society.[95] A new moratorium on some scale provides an opportunity for strategic pause while the nation and its leaders figure out what to do with a problem that is not likely to go away on its own.

Limit Numbers from certain nations – Completely opening the Golden Door to America and completely closing the Golden Door are on opposite sides of the control spectrum, and thus have equally low chances of being enacted by Congress. Limiting numbers of immigrants from certain nations is a compromise. Building on the idea of a moratorium on all immigration, which is politically infeasible, an alternative could be to place strict limitations on immigrants from certain countries. This idea has been tried before in the United States, but for largely xenophobic or isolationist reasons. Perhaps now is the time to try the idea again for more moral and practical reasons, the protection of national power elements of economy and diplomacy and the well-being of the American society.

With the explosive growth of diasporas within the United States, the statistics show which nationalities are contributing to the diaspora formation. These countries could be targeted

---

[95] Stein, 22.

for decrease immigration for a specific, limited amount of time, allowing the diasporas already in place to be integrated in to American society. After a certain amount of time and progress, the limitations on targeted nations could be lifted so as to allow for equality with other, non-targeted nations.

Deny citizenship to US born children of illegal immigrants – As discussed previously, anchor babies, or babies born to illegal aliens in the US, begin a chain of legal immigration that allow a few countries to unfairly dominate legal immigration well into the future.[96] Also shown earlier, immigrants, both legal and illegal, are increasingly forming diasporas across America. Granting automatic citizenship to any baby born in America perpetuates the assimilation problem as parents who are illegally in the United States are allowed to stay simply because they had a baby born in the United States. Denying birthright citizenship to children of illegal aliens removes one of the incentives for large-scale immigration to the United States.

Limit numbers based on the available government resources and financial capacity for absorbing immigrants – In 1986 Congress passed the 1986 Immigration and Reform Control Act, seeking to limit population movement into the United States. The Act especially targeted illegal immigration which seemed to be causing massive economic problems. During the 1990's, immigration was restricted even further by imposing severe penalties for undocumented migration and narrowing political and economic rights for immigrants who had neither citizenship or a green card. However, as shown earlier, these attempts failed to stem the rising tide of immigration.

One way to finally stem at least the flow of legal immigration to the United States would be to follow an example set by Canada. Canadian in-migration is determined by the Canadian government's estimates of the available government resources and financial capacity for

---

[96] J.D. Hayworth, *Whatever It Takes* (Washington, D.C.: Regnery Publishing, Inc., 2006), 185.

absorbing immigrants. The three qualifications for legal migration are family reunification, refugee status and financial status. Those immigrants that arrive with sufficient financial resources so they are not a burden on the state are more readily accepted. This approach could be used by the United States in the same manner. If an immigrant is deemed to be more of a drain on the economic and social systems than he/she is a benefit, then admittance is denied. This would eliminate the need to target specific nations and prevent the appearance of favoritism in the United States' immigration policy.[97]

Zero net immigration – The idea of zero net immigration grew out of the perceived need to negate the effect of immigration on population growth. This theory has been shown to be only partially effective due to the fact people tend to immigrate to the United States during their child-bearing years and emigrate only after much of their adult life has been spent in the United States working and raising a family.[98] The idea, however, does have some merit when viewed from the perspective of diaspora formation.

If a trailing average for the previous five years of emigration were used to set the limit of immigrants for the next five years, then at the very least, the explosive growth in diasporas would be diminished. Even if setting total immigration equal to total emigration is not politically feasible, perhaps using the formula for only targeted nationalities would still be effective in reducing the impacts of diasporas, by reducing or eliminating their growth. The limitations on immigrants from targeted nations would allow time for diasporas to be integrated into society.

Raise the cost of immigration – As discussed in Chapter 3, the cost of worldwide transportation is increasingly cheaper, removing a major barrier not only to immigration, but also to frequent return to the homeland. This ability to return often enables immigrants to maintain ties to the

---

[97] Ness, 71.
[98] Leon Bouvier, et al. "Zero Net International Migration," Center for International Studies, http://www.cis.org/articles/1995/back195.html, last accessed 12 February 2007.

homeland, aiding the propagation of diasporas. One thing is for certain: the cost of international transport will not increase in the coming years. Odds are, the cost will continue to decrease. With this in mind, there needs to be an artificial monetary hurdle placed in the way of coming and going. The hurdle can take the form of some kind of entry/exit tariff that would only apply to non-citizens of the United States. Of course, there would need to be tourism exemptions to prevent a decline in the lucrative tourist industry, but this is an issue of detail, not substance.

The tariff rate structure would be tied to initial entry to the United States for the purpose of immigrating and also tied to the length of visa requested. The tariff would apply each time an immigrant arrived back in the United States until the immigrant achieved American citizenship. At a minimum this would ensure that immigrants come here with the idea of staying and becoming American citizens. Other fees could be applied as well to other visas, such as student visas, but the taxing of student visas could actually cause a larger backlash against the United States. Student visas are a desirable way to get other nations' citizens to come to the United States to receive higher education. Student visas are a win-win situation for the United States as the students either become product citizens of the United States or return to their home country carrying the message of liberty, freedom, and equality they experienced while a student in the United States.

INTEGRATION INTO AMERICAN SOCIETY

President Bush also noted in his most recent State of the Union Address, "We need to uphold the great tradition of the melting pot the welcomes and assimilates new arrivals."[99] The recent problem of diaspora growth comes not from the lack of welcoming, but from the lack of assimilation. Pat Buchanon claims that the "great American Melting Pot is no longer melting…,"[100] an obvious reference to diaspora formation. Assimilation of immigrants is the next vital step in mitigating diasporas. If a nation's citizens are not "enjoined to love their country, to revere its institutions, to salute its flag, to support its sporting teams, to fight and die for it in war",[101] then the nation will become nothing more than a conglomeration of ethnic groups residing with no national identity or patriotism. The United States must assimilate its immigrants into an American society, with its own customs, cultures, beliefs, and identity.

Forbidding dual citizenship – This is an easy fix for Congress. The reasons behind it are more complex. It has been shown there is a desire for diaspora members to maintain a strong relationship with the homeland. There also is a strong desire to eventually return to the homeland. But is there a relationship between diaspora formation and dual-citizenship? This question is answered by Stanley Renshon in *The 50% American*.

The United States does not keep any records on the dual-citizenship status either of its citizens or of arriving immigrants, so exact numbers are not possible. However, it is possible to look at the countries that provide the vast pool of immigrants to the United States and whether or not those countries allow and/or encourage dual-citizenship. Of the top twenty sending nations, all but China, Cuba, and South Korea allow dual-citizenship. The rest of the top twenty appears to be a veritable "who's who" of diasporas within the United States, with five Latin American (Mexico far and away leads the pack) countries in the top ten, and the other five being Asian countries.[102] Even more telling are the raw numbers of immigrants from dual-citizenship

---

[99] President George W. Bush State of the Union Address to Combined Session of Congress, 23 January 2007, http://www.whitehouse.gov/news/releases/2007/01/20070123-2.html, last accessed 24 January 2007.
    [100] Pat Buchanon, "American Needs a Time Out on Immigration", see Barbour, ed., 32.
    [101] Robin Cohen, "Diasporas and the Nation-State: From Victims to Challengers", *International Affairs*, Vol. 72, No. 3, 1996, 518.
    [102] Renshon, 9.

countries. In the previous decade, an average of 85% of immigrants to the United States was from dual-citizenship-allowing countries.[103]

English as the national language – Unlike the waves of previous immigrants from Europe and Asia, significant numbers of Hispanics in the United States have demanded equal language rights.[104] At a press conference after the London terrorist bombing, British Prime Minister Tony Blair said, "You've got people who may be here…twenty years or more who still don't speak English. That worries me…because I think there's a separateness there that may be unhealthy."[105] It is just as unhealthy in America. One sure way to assimilate people into America is to learn to speak and understand English fluently. Diasporas, especially the larger ones in big cities such as Los Angeles and Miami, enable immigrants to live daily life speaking only the language of their homeland. Families should no doubt be allowed to speak whatever language they choose at home, and students should be able to pursue foreign language fluency in school. However, a complex, modern society such as the United States requires a common language, and that language must be English in the United States. Besides establishing English as the national language, Congress could also work with state and local officials to fund English classes for any immigrant wishing to improve his/her English skills in preparation for citizenship.

Pledge of Allegiance in schools – The Pledge of Allegiance may seem like a small thing to say, but when done properly, the Pledge can be a powerful tool in integration into American society. While several countries require an "Oath of Allegiance" for many of its government jobs, the United States is the only nation to advocate the recitation of a Pledge of Allegiance by all of its citizens, including children.[106] Many American ideals are contained within the Pledge, such as

---

[103] Ibid, 12.
[104] Cohen, "Diasporas and the Nation-State", 519.
[105] Hayworth, 187.
[106] A Google search for "Pledge of Allegiance" of the internet conducted 12 March 2007 returned only results referencing the United States. Additionally, Wikipedia references only the United States when

the existence of a higher being, the promise of allegiance, republican form of government, liberty and justice for all. While many nations have some or all of these ideals, the saying the American pledge symbolizes one's commitment and beliefs to the ideals contained therein, and to the United States and its people as a whole. The pledge, reinforced by citizenship classes, helps immigrants to understand that they are part of something special, with civic rights and responsibilities to support the democracy of the United States.

National service – Many nations have compulsory military service for their young men. This is an idea worth exploring. There are already procedures in place for foreign nationals to join the US military and reduce the time required to become an American citizen. Compulsory military service for immigrants as a condition of citizenship does have its limitations. However, if, instead of compulsory military service for immigrants, the idea of national service was expanded to include other departments such as USAID, the State Department, or even non-profit international aid organizations based in the United States, then an enormous amount of immigrants could be absorbed and included. Serving the nation is a sure-fire way to integrate an immigrant into society. It is an opportunity for the immigrant to learn the ideals of the nation, internalize them, and carry them forward to peoples of other nations. Once a required period of service was complete, the immigrant could then become a citizen of the United States and remain. If, however, the immigrant chose not to complete the requisite national service, then he/she would be asked to return to their country of origin.

The United States would benefit immeasurably from such a system. First, many of the hard-to-fill lower-level positions in the Departments of State and Defense would have a new found employment pool. Additionally, the ability to intervene militarily, economically, or

---

searching for "Pledge of Allegiance." Several countries require an oath of citizenship when immigrants apply to become citizens. However, no other countries can be found with an official Pledge of Allegiance for all citizens sponsored by the central government of that nation.

diplomatically would be enhanced by a deeper pool of ethnic talent from around the world. Finally, the national power of the United States would be enhanced as the nation would be seen as one which upholds its ideals and extends a welcome to peoples of all nations by integrating them into society through service to the nation.

IMPLICATIONS FOR THE FUTURE

The United States reached its current lofty status as the world's only superpower by providing unparalleled personal freedoms and abundant economic opportunity. The United States has opened its doors and invited immigrants from all over the world to join the Great Melting Pot. In return, the United States has asked of immigrants to learn the country's language, culture, and political practices. This was intended to orient immigrants to their new home and become American. Leaving life and homeland behind has always been difficult. Yet, generations of immigrants have thought the sacrifice worthwhile.[107] From this, many cultures have become one nation. However, recently the immigration process into the United States has been undergoing changes, with potentially devastating negative effects.

Trends in international migration from countries of lesser economic advantage to those of more economic advantage can only be seen to continue in the coming years. The ability to move back and forth between one's home nation and that of a new country will also continue to be easier and easier. As more and more immigrants arrive in the United States and form diasporas, the difficulties of social and economic integration become greater and greater. The United States cannot afford to continue business as usual with its current immigration policies. Diasporas are increasing at an explosive rate, and with them, the rate of the nation's GDP leaving the country in

---

[107] Renshon, 158.

the form of remittances is exploding. Remittances already vastly exceed the amount of official development aid by nearly two times as much, and this difference will continue to grow.

The ability of diasporas to affect changes in both US policy and home-nation policy will increase and cause the ability of the United States to apply economic aid and military power to decrease. As the world becomes more and more globalized and interdependent, the United States will be forced to reduce its dependence on the military element of national power. Wars will become too costly to the international order, having far-reaching effects on other than the two belligerent nations. In light of diminishing opportunities to use military power, the United States must maintain the economic and diplomatic advantage it has gained over the years. Diasporas undermine both the economic and diplomatic instruments of national power.

FUTURE STUDY

The suggestions for immigration policy reform and mitigation of the negative effects of diasporas are not intended to be implemented without further study of their impact. Solving one problem may very well create unforeseen problems far worse than the one just solved. Serious study of second and third order effects must be undertaken to insure the US is as least aware of the existence of unwanted effects, even if the effects are acceptable in the solution.

One such second order effect of suspending all immigration, even for only a short period of time, could actually enable the formation of diasporas. For example, if immigration is suspended, and the US border with Mexico has not been sufficiently secured, then illegal immigration across that border will likely explode. Immigrants, who might otherwise enter the US legally, would be forced to enter illegally and, as a result, seek to remain out of mainstream American society. The immigrant would necessarily be attracted to Mexican diasporas within the US as their only source of support. This effect would perpetuate Mexican and/or Latino diaspora formation and defeat the purpose of suspending immigration in the first place.

Another possible second order effect of dampening the impact of diasporas could be a possible public outcry from US citizens, diaspora members, or other nations who rely on the ability of people to immigrate into the US. The political power of diasporas has already been demonstrated to be capable of influencing state actions. The impact of one million Asians in Los Angeles or one million Latinos in Miami all rising as one against decisions made by the government affecting immigration could quite possibly outweigh any benefits of taking action, or even destabilize two or more of America's largest world cities.

While the second or third order effects of taking affirmative action to mitigate diaspora formation are not clear, the need to take action is clear. Immigrants seeking entry into the United States for the purpose of taking advantage of the thriving economy, superior public services, and American good faith cannot be allowed to continue unabated. There is a huge money drain from both the exported GDP and the drain on public services that must be stopped. America's military might is being mitigated all across the world as potential foes find ever-increasing ingenious ways to counter conventional military power. The US must be able to maintain its diplomatic and economic power if it wants to remain a superpower, if not the world's only superpower. It is in the US' vital national interest to solve the growing problems created by diaspora formation within its borders.

BIBLIOGRAPHY

Anzovin, Steven. *The Problem of Immigration.* New York: H.W. Wilson, 1985.

Barbour, Scott. *Immigration Policy.* San Diego, Calif.: Greenhaven Press, 1995.

"Borders and Law Enforcement". US Embassy in Mexico, http://mexico.usembassy.gov/mexico/ebordermechs.html, last accessed 15 February 2007.

Bouvier, Leon, et al. "Zero Net International Migration," Center for International Studies, http://www.cis.org/articles/1995/back195.html, last accessed 12 February 2007.

Bush, George W., State of the Union Address to Combined Session of Congress, 23 January 2007, http://www.whitehouse.gov/news/releases/2007/01/20070123-2.html, last accessed 24 January 2007.

Carrington, William J., and Enrica Detragiache. "How Extensive is the Brain Drain?", Finance and Development Quarterly, Vol. 36, No. 2, 1999. International Monetary Fund, http://www.imf.org/external/pubs/ft/fandd/1999/06/carringt.htm, last accessed 15 February 2007.

Castles, Stephen, and Mark J. Miller. *The Age of Migration : International Population Movements in the Modern World.* New York: Guilford Press, 1993.

Clark, William A.V. "Immigration and California Communities", February 1999, Center for Immigration Studies, http://www.cis.org/articles/1999/back299.html, last accessed 15 February 2007.

Cohen, Robin. "Diasporas and the Nation-State: From Victims to Challengers", *International Affairs*, Vol. 72, No. 3, 1996.

Cohen, Robin. *Global Diasporas: An Introduction.* Seattle: University of Washington Press, 1997.

Collier, Paul. "Economic Causes of Civil Conflict and Their Implications for Policy". World Bank, http://www.worldbank.org/research/conflict/papers/civilconflict.pdf, last accessed 15 February 2007.

Davies, Wendy. *Closing the Borders.* New York: Thomson Learning, 1995.

DellaPergola, Sergio, Yehezkel Dror, and Shalom S. Wald. *Annual Assessment 2005: A Rapidly Changing World.* Jerusalem: Jewish People Policy Planning Institute, 2006.

"Destination America". PBS Website, www.pbs.org/destinationamerica/usim_qz1b.html, last accessed 10 March 2007.

Divine, Robert A. *American Immigration Policy, 1924-1952.* New Haven: Yale University Press, 1957.

Dudley, William. *Illegal Immigration.* San Diego, CA: Greenhaven Press, 2002.

Easterly, William. *The White Man's Burden.* New York: The Penguin Press, 2005.

Ember, Carol R., Melvin Ember, and Ian A. Skoggard. *Encyclopedia of Diasporas : Immigrant and Refugee Cultures Around the World.* New York: Springer, 2005.

Federal Motor Carrier Safety Administration, http://www.fmcsa.dot.gov/images/us-mexico-border.jpg, last accessed 15 February 2007.

Fong, Timothy P. *The First Suburban Chinatown.* Philadelphia: Temple University Press, 1994.

Friedman, Thomas. *The Lexus and the Olive Tree.* New York: Random House, Inc., 2000.

Future Phone Corporation, http://www.futurephone.com, last accessed 15 February 2007.

Gilbert, Geoffrey. *World Population : A Reference Handbook.* Santa Barbara ; Denver: Abc-Clio, 2001.

Globalization and World Cities Website, http://www.lboro.ac.uk/gawc/citymap.html, last accessed 15 February 2007.

"Glossary", U.S. Citizenship and Immigration Services, http://www.uscis.gov/graphics/glossary3.html, last accessed 22 October 2007.

Hayes, David. "Free Overseas Calls," *Kansas City Star,* 29 October 2006, sec. D.

Hayworth, J. D., and Joe Eule. *Whatever it Takes : Illegal Immigration, Border Security, and the War on Terror.* Washington, D.C.: Regnery, 2006.

Heliwell, John F. *How Much Do National Borders Matter?* Washington, D.C.: Brookings Institute Press, 1998.

"Hominid Fossil Sites", http://www.handprint.com/LS/ANC/disp.html, last accessed 15 February 2007.

"International Monetary Fund GDP Statistics". International Monetary Fund Website, http://www.imf.org/external/pubs/ft/weo/2006/02/data/index.aspx, last accessed 14 February 2007.

Isaac, Julius. *Economics of Migration.* New York: Oxford University Press, 1947.

Jenks, Jeremiah Whipple, William Jett Lauck, and Rufus Daniel Smith. *The Immigration Problem: A Study of American Immigration Conditions and Needs.* 6th , rev. and enl. ed. New York: Funk & Wagnalls, 1926.

Keck, Margaret and Kathryn Sikkink *Activists Beyond Borders.* Ithaca, NY: Cornell University Press, 1998.

Leff, Laurel. "The Los Angeles Melting Pot", *Immigrants, Refugees, and U.S. Policy.* New York: The H.W. Wilson Company, 1981.

Leitsinger, Miranda. "Brain Drain: Flight from Puerto Rico," *Kansas City Star,* 28 October 2006, sec. 1A.

Levine, Herbert M. *Immigration.* Austin, Texas: Raintree Steck-Vaughn, 1998.

Levinson, David. *Ethnic Groups Worldwide : A Ready Reference Handbook.* Phoenix, Ariz.: Oryx Press, 1998.

Long, Robert Emmet. *Immigration.* New York: H.W. Wilson, 1996.

Long, Robert Emmet. *Immigration to the U.S.* New York: H.W. Wilson, 1992.

Martin v. Wilkes, United States Supreme Court, 1875.

Morris, Milton D., and Albert Mayio. *Curbing Illegal Immigration.* Washington, D.C.: Brookings Institution, 1982.

Ness, Immanuel, and James Ciment. *Encyclopedia of Global Population and Demographics.* Armonk, NY: Sharpe Reference, 1999.

Portrait of the USA". United States Department of State, http://usinfo.state.gov/ usa/infousa/facts/factover; last accessed 15 February 2007.

Reimers, David M. *Still the Golden Door : The Third World Comes to America.* 2nd ed. New York: Columbia University Press, 1000; 1992.

"Remittance Trends 2006". World Bank, http://siteresources.worldbank.org/ NEWS/MiscContent/21124588/mad.pdf, last accessed 15 February 2007.

Renshon, Stanley Allen. *The 50% American : Immigration and National Identity in an Age of Terror.* Washington, D.C.: Georgetown University Press, 2005.

Russell, Cheryl. *Demographics of the U.S. : Trends and Projections.* 2nd ed. Ithaca, N.Y.: New Strategist Publications, 2003.

Scott, Franklin Daniel. *World Migration in Modern Times.* Englewood, N.J.: Prentice-Hall, 1968.

Segal, Ronald. *The Black Diaspora.* New York: Farrar, Straus and Giroux, 1995.

Sheffer, Gabriel, editor. *Modern Diasporas in International Politics.* London: Croom Helm, 1986.

"State and Country Quick Facts", Census Bureau, http://quickfacts.census.gov/qfd/states/06/06037.html, last accessed 15 February 2007.

Taft, Donald Reed. *Human Migration : A Study of International Movements.* New York: Ronald Press, 1936.

Taft, Donald Reed, and Richard Robbins. *International Migrations : The Immigrant in the Modern World.* New York: Ronald Press, 1000.

Tanton, John H. "The End of the Migration Epoch", *The Social Contract*, Vol. IV, No. 3, 1995. Demographic, Environmental, and Security Issues Project, http://desip.igc.org/1800.html and http://desip.igc.org/2050.html, last accessed 15 February 2007.

Teitelbaum, Michael S., American Assembly, and Myron Weiner. *Threatened Peoples, Threatened Borders : World Migration and U.S. Policy.* New York: W.W. Norton, 1995.

"USA Pop Clock". United States Census Bureau, www.census.gov/population/www/popclockus.html, last accessed 15 February 2007.

Van Hear, Nicholas. *New Diasporas : The Mass Exodus, Dispersal and Regrouping of Migrant Communities.* Seattle, WA: University of Washington Press, 1998.

Vertovec, Steven. "The Political Importance of Diasporas", June 1, 2005. Migration Information Source, http://www.migrationinformation.org/Feature/display.cfm?ID=313, last accessed 8 December 2006.

"Visa Remittance Solutions". Visa Corporation, http://corporate.visa.com/ pd/pdf/remittance.pdf, last accessed 15 February 2007.

Whitaker, Matt. "Immigrants Send Billions Abroad Each Year", November 14, 2006. Apostille US, http://apostille.us/news/immigrants send billions abroad each year now banks want a piece of the action.shtml.

www.ingramcontent.com/pod-product-compliance
Lightning Source LLC
Chambersburg PA
CBHW082149290526
45794CB00008B/3218